David Enker

Phantom Parents

Memoir of an adoptee

Phantom Parents

Memoir of an adoptee

First global edition - May 2023

All artwork - Copyright © 2023 David Enker
Haarlem, The Netherlands
www.davidenker.com

Crowdfunding by voordekunst.nl

Self-publishing powered by Amsterdam Academy Press
www.amsterdamacademy.com

InDesign corrections: Lisa Hall, www.lemonberry.com

Proofreading/editing: Kristin Anderson, www.kristininholland.com

Printed and bound by IngramSpark, www.ingramspark.com

ISBN 9789090369440
NUR 303

To
Ailish & Yaron

Contents

ESTD   D E   1970
PHANTOM PARENTS
MEMOIR OF AN ADOPTEE
A GRAPHIC NOVEL
200 PAGES
FULL COLOR EDITION
HAARLEM, AMSTERDAM
LONDON, DETROIT, TEL AVIV
PUBLISHED
2023
DAVID ENKER

Introduction

This book has been made possible through crowdfunding. From an early age, I enjoyed writing and drawing, and dreamed about creating my own book one day. The process of collating this collection of short stories, many of them years old, has come at a difficult time in my life. Recently I was diagnosed with a life-changing illness, which has given some urgency to this long-standing dream to publish my work.

Through the perspective of an adoptee, this book is an exploration of life, its highs and lows, and even the absurd. The stories are loosely based on real events, and although the names of most involved have been changed, it is as close to a memoir as it gets.

David Dylan Jona Enker
Haarlem, April 2023

You will find more of these in this book. Use the camera on your smartphone to scan and you will be directed to an Instagram reel, a short videoclip with a soundtrack. You don't need an account.

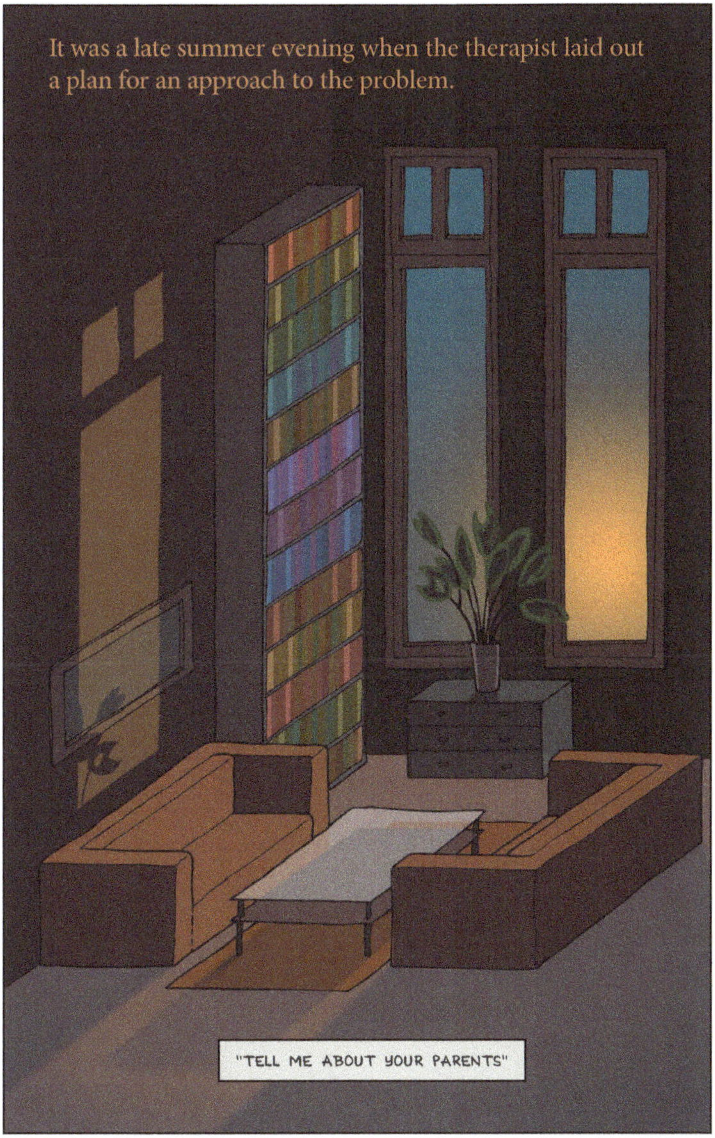

It was a late summer evening when the therapist laid out
a plan for an approach to the problem.

1

From Amsterdam to The Hague

The 1970s
A period of dreams

AMSTERDAM, SPRING 1970

BLA!

BLA!

?
BLA!

UNIVERSITEIT VAN AMSTERDAM
BLA!

FEMINIST BAR
BLA?..

?
?
?

CAREER
MOTHER

5 YEARS LATER

Just Like Mine

The sand nestled itself between my toes. I had never been to the beach with my birth mother before. Usually when I visited her, we would go to the park or just cycle around the city, with me on the little seat on the front of her bike, my eyes navigating our way.

This time, however, she took me on a short train trip to the coast on a mid-weekday somewhere in May. She smelled kind of funny – a mixture of a rosy perfume and cigarettes – and there was something strangely familiar about her skin with its slightly pale complexion.

Back home, with my 'adoptive' mother, it always smelled like fresh bread, as we lived on the second floor above a bakery. But that day when my birth mother came and collected me, it was the first time I realised that she, despite her constant smoking, actually smelled very nice and not just because of her perfume. For the first time in my life I felt a kinship, and more than ever before I was interested where she would take me.

She chose the train compartment filled with a bluish layer of smoke and lots of grownups. My polite coughs went unnoticed. We rode in silence until the dunes appeared from behind the clouds. My birth mother started talking, something about when I was a baby or something, but my attention strayed to the windows that had a picture on them of a red circle with a hand holding a bottle.

We walked from the station and passed some grey, cubical houses as we headed towards the beach. I started running towards the sand, leaving my sandals behind. I had been to the beach before, just not here and not with her. She slowly took off her flip-flops and smiled at me as she walked in my direction across the sand.

I ran towards the sea, cold at first, but warmer on a shimmy. I saw my birth mother standing just before the shore. I looked back toward the horizon. The sea had a gradient of colour that went from a dark muddy brown between my toes to a grey blue, which ended abruptly in the dark line of the horizon. Greyish-white waves capped the surface of the water. Above it all, a pale blue sky was ever watching, filled with laughing seagulls flying in formation in front of an impressive army of woolly clouds.

I walked back to her. She was now sitting in the sand, smoking a cigarette, looking at me with a frown on her face, but she was also completely still, seemingly far away and deep in thought.

She started talking again, but I noticed that my feet, wet from the sea, were covered in damp little balls of sand that I could gently rub off with my hands. Now and then my mother would stop talking and I would look at her, with her blue veins slightly visible through her skin, and her blonde hair, just like mine.

The End of the World

The ground beneath the feet of the quiffed reporter and his talking dog is heating up so much that the asphalt is melting. At the same time, a mysterious star appears in the evening sky next to the big dipper. The curious reporter decides to call Star Watch.

It is Friday, late afternoon. The smell of onion meatballs and gravy fills the air, together with the sound of talking heads on the kitchen radio. I close my door and continue reading my comic book.

Dinner is served. My brother has just laid the table, and from my elevated chair, I can almost see everything on it. My mother puts the mashed potatoes on my plate, creates a hole in the middle and pours some gravy in it, together with a couple of meatballs. On the table is a bowl of brussels sprouts. I say I don't want them as they smell like my brother's farts. Despite my protest I get them anyway, accompanied by some cucumber salad and my brother's sniggering.

My mother says something, to which my brother answers in a mumble. My sister sighs and moves to the other side of the table. They all look so tall and grown up. My brother is seven years older than me and he is from another planet. He talks strangely, and his room smells like sweaty socks. My sister is nine years older and is unfathomable to me but at least she smells nice. She loves the colour purple, which you can see on her clothes and her room. She's out of the house most of the time and I think she will be moving to The Hague soon, to live with our father.

My sister is kind to me, and I will miss her. It was she who insisted that I stay with the family. My adoption was never formalised, so when my birth mother finished her study and wanted me back, my sister said 'No, he's my cute little brother'.

After dinner we do the dishes together. My brother washes and I dry. He turns the channel on the radio and loud music floods the kitchen. He puts some water in his long blond hair and throws it backwards as he starts singing along with the song on the radio. He grabs the scrubber and holds it in front of his mouth as if it is a microphone and starts making weird, uncontrollable movements with his body. I laugh and he asks me to join him. My sister jabs him in the ribs and grabs the microphone. As we sing and dance, I look at the kitchen door to the balcony. It is pitch dark outside, so you can clearly see our reflections in the glass door.

Magic

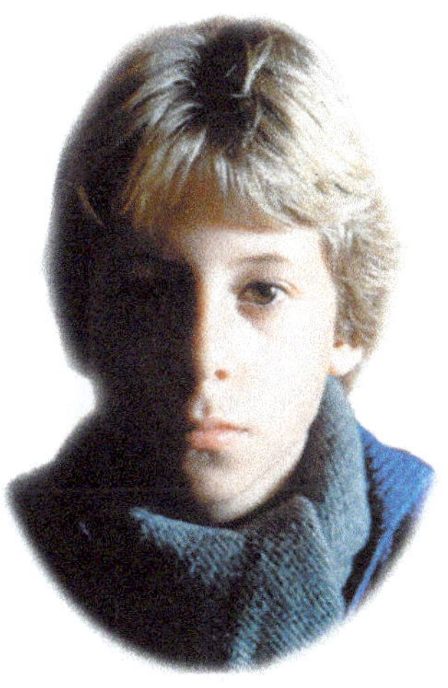

My serious stare, aged 10
Photo: Joop Polder

When I was around ten years old, we moved from Amsterdam to The Hague to start afresh: *a new life.*

Now it was just my mother and me. We stayed with a friend of the family until we could find a place of our own. Both my older sister and brother were living with our father elsewhere in The Hague.

Things had not worked out in Amsterdam; the work and living situation had become untenable. I recall how distressed my mother was about my walking through the inner-city and Vondelpark just to go to school. In my mind it was a huge kids' fantasy, but in her mind, it was a playground for muggers and flashers.

We moved when my mother finally managed to get some work in The Hague, a city my mother new well, as we had all lived there eight years earlier, before my parents divorced.

We now found ourselves in a small, second-floor apartment, a five-minute's walk from my new school. My mother's friend was rarely home, so it was mostly just the two of us and a resident white cat.

My class in the new school was a lot smaller than the one I went to in Amsterdam, which felt kind of pleasant, but I was keen to be home as I was not acquainted with any of the new kids yet.

One Wednesday afternoon, my mother and her friend were both at home. The two of them were talking about grownup things. My toys and books were in the guest room that my mother and I shared. I was really into 'The Wonderful World of Henry Sugar' by Roald Dahl.

I wished I could see through things, just like the character from the book could. Or more precisely, that I could use my mind, through sheer willpower, to control things and people to do whatever I wanted them to do. I tried using mind control on our playing cards. I so badly wanted to believe I had this power, that I convinced myself I could indeed see through the cards.

With a desire to demonstrate my newfound gift to my mother, I went to the living room where they were still talking in adult voices. I interrupted them by announcing my magical gift and used the playing cards to show them my trick. My mother and her friend laughed and applauded, which confirmed my suspicion that the trick had failed.

My mother pulled me to sit next to her and continued with her chat. While sitting there I noticed her trousers had long creases in them that intrigued me. I could not resist reaching out and giving the fabric a good pinch.

My mother yelped.

'What did you do that for?' she asked.

'I just wanted to know if you were real,' I said, 'and so you are.' And then I bowed.

She laughed again, but this time it was genuine. Then she kissed me.

'Magic,' she said, as she looked at me a little longer.

Naked

I enter the hospital room and there he is, sitting up straight in his bed with his bald head hanging low in his hands. I can't see his face and his thin, long fingers reveal his bones. My father doesn't seem to notice me.

My mother and my father's second, current wife are outside in the hallway, holding guard. They close the door behind me. I get closer to him and whisper his name. Slowly he raises his head.

There is no way you can prepare for something like this. The illness has eaten away his temples and cheeks, his eyes are bulging marbles hanging in caves next to his still prominent but thinned nose. Not much is left of his neck and his teeth are visible through the paper-thin skin of his jaws.

Yet upon noticing me, his eyes light up. He says my name and a faint smile appears on his thin lips. He says something about how glad he is that I came to visit. I keep on looking at him, knowing it will be the last time.

Here is the man who adopted me as a baby, he along with my mother, one of the two women now sitting outside in the hallway. Although they divorced when I was only two years old, he continued to play an important role in my life. In the summer I would often spend my holidays with him, his second

wife, and their son. I remember him being very at ease with himself, walking around the house naked, visitors or not. He would be sitting on some rattan chair reading a book and I would be wondering how painful that must have felt without clothes on. I would often read something from his comic book collection, and find my father within the characters. Robert Crumb, for example, prompted me to think of my father as one of his characters called Mister Natural, a serene fellow with his infinite meditation sessions.

That was only a couple of years ago and now here I am, not even 16 years old, looking at Mister Natural in his hospital bed soon to be rolling out his meditation rug for eternity. I know how much he has been in pain the last couple of months and how he must be delirious from the morphine in his body. But that faint smile he just gave me was real, and so is the glimmer in his eyes as he looks at me. It is as if he is now more naked than ever before and all I can see is his soul, smiling at me forever.

The Man with the Hat

Maybe the man with the hat is my biological father, hiding behind his newspaper four seats away in the train. I spoke with him over the phone a couple of weeks ago, but I can't picture him, as all I have is this tiny photograph of him from long ago. His face is pushed half out of the picture frame by me, a two-year-old, apprehensive, white-haired chubber. His half-face is dressed with a neatly trimmed beard and metal-framed glasses. He seems absent, as if he knows this will be the last time he sees me.

It is over fifteen years since that picture was taken, and I am on my way to meet him for the first time. I am holding the small square photograph my birth mother only recently gave to me, as if it is a secret file released by a collapsed regime.

A few months ago, at a birthday gathering, I asked my birth mother who my biological father was. She wrote his name on a piece of paper together with his phone number. After that, she sent the picture by post.

I look at it again. It really is tiny. My birth mother must have taken it, which might explain his absent look as well. It really didn't work well between the two of them.

Who is he? What does he look like now? He could also be on his way here to meet me, coming from the opposite direction.

Will he recognise me? Parents should have a natural gift for that, surely.

The man with the hat looks at me. Nervously I look away. It isn't him. I can tell, because I don't feel anything, at least not recognition.

The empty landscape passes by outside. It is a mild November day and the low sun casts a warm orange-yellow light through the train carriage. A bunch of kids about my age are chatting and laughing, but I don't hear them.

Upon arrival at the station I merge into the crowd. It is a Saturday, and people seem very excited. I get into the tram and manage to get a seat. By now, it has turned dark outside.

Inside the tram I see all these faces. A little kid is looking at me while his mum is staring outside. Can he tell I am on my way to meet my biological father? I must look suspicious. No need to worry, I tell myself, soon all will be clear. Whether my biological father is a wealthy man, an intellectual, an old hippy or some bum, it shouldn't matter. At least I know then, and I can move on.

A sudden wind blows in my face when I turn the corner into his street. The tall apartment buildings on one side of the street are overlooking a canal and there is an open space on the other side. The rhythmic streetlights throw a dark orange light onto the row houses. My biological father lives in one of them. I look again at the piece of paper my mother gave to me and check the house number.

Door after door, window after window, the number slowly increases. I finally reach the right number. It is not a door facing the street, rather it is a portal with steps upwards towards a little hallway with four doors next to each other. His name is on the right-hand door. I put the piece of paper away and try to imagine what he looks like. I am more nervous than ever before, but manage to push the doorbell.

At first it remains quiet. I swallow. Then, a gentle ruffle sounds and a hall light goes on. The footsteps I hear reveal a nature not that different to my own. The door opens and the bright light blinds me just coming from the dark outside. I can see the silhouette of a person my size and slowly the face of the man from the picture appears on it. The voice I recognize from the telephone asks me if I had a good journey and whether I prefer tea, or coffee.

Oma Z

It is somewhere in the mid-nineties when I visit my grandmother in The Hague; my birth mother's mother. I am in my mid-twenties. Normally I would see her at a family gathering, like for her birthday, and the whole family would be there. But this is not her birthday; it is just me and her. Her reputation as an overbearing mother, a bitter complainer, and a husband divorcer is all gone now, and it is just the two of us. Her apartment is on the 10th floor of a block built for seniors. Yellow parakeets are flying around the room and her parrot mimics our conversation from its cage.

She offers me a cigarette from a silver mug. I decline, not because I don't smoke, but because they are ultra-light tasteless cigarettes. My grandmother lights one up. I look at the pictures on top of her TV; standing up, framed, is a picture of her in her twenties, dressed in a fur coat, stylishly smoking a cigarette. Sitting next to her is a handsome man in a light suit with curly hair who is not my grandfather.

'I've always wondered who that was, Oma Z.' That's what I call her.

'That was Albert, the love of my life,' she says while puffing out some smoke.

'Who was he?' I ask, thinking: why not my grandfather?

She tells me the story of Albert and Indonesia, the outbreak of the Second World War; that although she had already met my grandfather, she favoured Albert. Albert was half Jewish and had some connection with Indonesia, which was still a Dutch colony at that time. Oma Z moved to Indonesia with him. They married and had a child, my aunt Edith, but the war followed them. They were incarcerated by the Japanese in a concentration camp, and Albert died there. My grandmother believed she was protected by guardian angels.

I imagine my young grandmother with a baby at her feet holding the vertical bars in the camp while angels hovered over her.

'Then what happened?' I ask.

'Once the Japanese were defeated and the camp was liberated, I returned with my young daughter to Holland. There I reconnected with your grandfather, who never stopped loving me throughout the war and he proposed to me.'

I imagine my grandfather going down on one knee in front of my grandmother still wearing her fur coat but with a child on her lap and a tear in her eye.

'Your grandfather was the hairiest man I have ever seen,' she says, and I think of how many men she must have seen. 'He was short and had hair all over his back.' There aren't any pictures of him in her apartment. In the other room there's an oval picture of me when I was about 12 years old, smiling and still tanned from a summer holiday.

'Your grandfather had returned from the war a parentless, broken man just as I had returned from Indonesia a widow. And that's how we reunited.'

'Holocaust!' the parrot yells.

'I hope you don't become a *lerner* like your grandfather,' Oma Z says.

'Lerner or learner?', I think. 'What do you mean?'

'That's a Jewish thing where a man is studying all day while his wife works. Your grandfather was like that; he studied and studied, mostly biblical stuff. I raised the children.'

She looks at me and lights another cigarette.

'You like to draw and such, comics and all. You clearly have a talent. Just don't waste it, that's all I can say. Otherwise you'll be sorry for the rest of your life.'

A month later I got a phone call she was dead.

This is not a Magritte

2

From The Hague
to Detroit

1993
A life-changing journey

Around Midnight

Diary Entry: The Hague, 28 June 1993

Just watched some TV and took a walk. Lovely sultry summer evening for a walk. Had to think about many things. Before the walk, I watched an episode of Cheers. Silly show really. But funny episode nevertheless. It was about the meaning of life (or lack of). For one person, the meaning of life could be to have nice shoes, for the other, family and stuff. Naturally during my walk, I was pondering *my* meaning.

Frasier, the psychologist in the show, argued that there is no point in asking this question. Whilst walking, thinking, and contemplating this question for some time, taking into account the screaming void I experience now and then, I had to concur.

On that same walk, I came up with a few principles for myself. When there isn't any important stuff to do, like being with a girl, travelling, working, or listening to music, etc., then go write, just like now, or do something physical. If there are problems, tell people around you: friends, a shrink, whatever; have a walk, and write. Do something. Doesn't matter what. Beware of dogmas though; always be prepared to look beyond yourself.

Writing isn't such a bad pastime. Maybe this is my meaning of life, maybe it isn't. But never lose hope.

During my walk, I also had to think about Le Penseur, The Thinker. 'I think, therefore I am'. Once there was a creature asking itself: 'But why …?' This question is one of the first things to distinguish us from animals. The beginning of man. A typical human trait to wonder and ponder. The search for meaning, a reason for things to happen. My feeling is that this 'thinking' causes a lot of misery. Maybe I just ask the wrong questions. We live in a society that was shaped by generations before us, and many predecessors asked themselves new questions in response to past explanations of things, and by doing so, extended our society into something more complex. Each new generation has to process more and more. The bureaucratic labyrinth of the collective mind keeps on expanding.

I also wondered: *Why?* Where do I come from? Why is there space? What is the beginning, what is the end? What is coincidence and why does it exist?

The more questions, the less answers. All these questions detached me more and more from my fellow human beings. I used to see myself as the thinker ('D. Enker' is like 'Th. Inker'), but I can't escape the feeling that since I've been thinking so much I have been 'going down' somewhat. Afterall, my grandmother warned me of 'The Thinker' trap.

Sometimes I wish total chaos would occur: no electricity, no communication, and the emergence of some kind of anarchy in which, no doubt, some really primal elements would manifest. It would be the end of bad TV shows and football. Smaller groups would start to form that would have to rely on instinct and feeling rather than rules and laws. I would be fine. In fact, I would be great!

My feelings aren't satisfied in this overly rational society. Are you healthy? Do sports. Are you smart? Go study. Earn money. Get a house. You are such a good learner! You are so handsome! So smart! Do something with it!

I prefer to find things out for myself. I might just be an *Average Joe* for all I know, but at least I give in to my inner voices, my mind, my heart, and my soul.

It seems as if a huge task lies ahead of me. My whole life I have felt different, as if I need to do something of the utmost importance. Something for humanity. Something truly essential.

I struggle to hold an interest in just one topic. Every time there seems to be something that stops me, like studying physics. I want to understand rational thinking. But when I more or less 'get' it, the challenge disappears. Now I feel like I need to follow my instincts more often, and rely more on my feelings. I believe my strength is there, even though I thought the same about my rational capabilities. If you rely on your feelings – maintaining self-confidence – without hiding from your true self, there is not much to lose, right?!

Sometimes people say if I apply myself, I can do well at university. But I felt imprisoned in what seemed to be a hyper-rational society bound by rules. When I was a teenager, I didn't know any better and just followed the easy way, that of the crowd, at least in part.

It is, however, very important to listen to your inner self, no matter how difficult that sometimes may seem. *Carl Jung* tells us about the treasures in our own subconscious, and I kind of *believe* in that (look at me … the 'believing atheist'). I know that I manage life better when I listen to my instincts. It feels like some sort of organism guides my actions other than myself, and that organism has a lot to do with fantasy, imagination, love, and sorrow.

Maybe I hide my emotions for fear of being hurt, and because of the presence of so much misery in the world (in my perception anyway). And 'being lived' rather than living:

A too tight schedule; not eating when you run out of time; going to bed when you aren't tired but falling asleep during class, etcetera, as a result of foisted norms, other people's values, or even your own rules. This can't be good for our wellbeing.

My escape from this torturous feeling is the ratio. At high school I changed from one day to the next, suddenly being very good at physics and mathematics, and I turned my back on my emotional world. Was it fear? The reason is not entirely clear.

It could have had something to do with my 'heritage' – my unclear family situation, absent fathers, expectations; my complex personality, being so goddamn unsure about everything one moment, but then overly sure the next; my lack of commitment (or is it lack of will?); experiences in my past (a difficult puberty, moving home so many times, damaged trust in some people) and who knows what else.

It's not easy returning to a more emotional state.

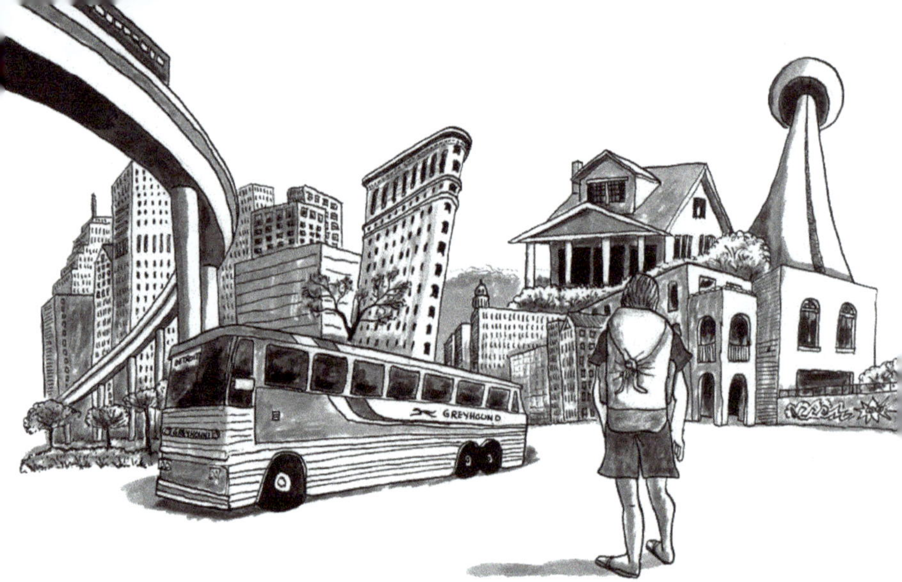

The North America Trip

Travelling through North America by Greyhound bus
August–September 1993

QR code for soundtrack

Baltimore, Wednesday, 18 August 1993,
22:10 local time

I arrived here eight days ago. Let's start from the beginning.

My mother joined me on the train from The Hague to Amsterdam–Schiphol airport, and waved me off. After passport control, I bought two film rolls and a Dutch newspaper. I boarded a small aircraft from Iceland Air filled with odd looking and even odder speaking people. I was on my way to America! Taking off was one of the most exciting moments of my life.

My seat was next to the window. It was sunny and the green and yellow patches of England were clearly visible below. There were some really cute stewardesses, and a cute Icelandic girl sat next to me, flanked by her mute boyfriend. Approaching Iceland was like approaching the moon, completely barren, with some Fuji-like mountains on top. I spent some time at Keflavik Airport, where I bought a cassette tape of Björk's debut album, even though I didn't bring my Walkman.

The next plane was as small as the first one, although this time I had an aisle seat. A little girl, around eleven year's old, was sitting next to me. This time it felt colder in the craft.

When we arrived at 'BWI' *(Baltimore-Washington International Airport)* I was checked by security. I had to provide the address of where I was staying and for how long. I reached the main arrivals hall, and my hosts hadn't arrived yet. Apparently, I was about an hour early. For me it was past midnight, even though it was only around seven o'clock in the evening. It was hot, humid, and bright outside – a very different climate from what I was used to. I was beginning to feel jet lag for the first time in my life. I spoke with some guy from 'DC', realising I had to get used to listening to and speaking American English. Then Jake walked in the hall.

Jake is the father of Sam, a guy I knew when I was around 12 or so, whom I came to visit. Our parents were friends. I hadn't seen Sam since he moved back to the US with his dad after his parents got divorced. His Dutch mom stayed in Holland. Jake, once a hippy street guitarist, was now working in a paint store and living with Jen, a woman working at the University of Maryland. I would be staying with Jake and Jen for the first couple of days before meeting up with Sam, who was currently busy; with what, I didn't know yet.

Jake, in his mid-forties, had hardly changed in the 10 years or so since I last saw him. He was a jovial, relatively short guy (I was now the same height), with curly shoulder-length hair, who slightly resembled Bob Dylan – including the hoarse voice. He was wearing a loose T-shirt, jeans, and sandals. He gave a nod to the guy I was chatting with and gestured for me to go outside, without that strange guy. Jen, whom I had never met before, was outside in the car. She seemed miles away from the laid-back hippy style that Jake had about him. She had a grey quiff and a permanent friendly smile on her face. She seemed more educated than Jake, but they had a good chemistry together. After we were introduced, we drove through Baltimore via the new harbour.

Jen drove us to *Pikesville*, a pleasant leafy suburb Northwest of Baltimore's city centre where they lived. I had imagined these suburbs would be much uglier, but was pleasantly surprised. There were no shops in their neighborhood, as everybody used cars to go to big malls. The suburb and surroundings reminded me a bit of Southern France, including the warm weather. Their area was made up of quiet lanes with wooden houses in different colours. Most of the homes were over a hundred years old.

Pikesville

Their red wooden house had a large front porch with a hammock on it, and was just as pretty as the surrounding homes. The interior was very large, with many rooms and a wide staircase. We went to the kitchen which had a typical humungous American fridge. Jake confessed that he had been smoking marijuana for the past 28 years, and immediately produced a salad bowl filled to the top with weed and started rolling a thin, pure joint. I was feeling the jet lag and the last thing I wanted was to smoke weed in a strange country, so when I saw my opportunity, I said I'd like to make it an early night. Jake led me to their TV room, which would be my room for the next few days.

I released my rucksack and turned on their little TV. Contrary to what I expected, they only had a couple of channels via an antenna. But on every channel there were ads every five minutes or so. One channel was called the '*Psychic Discovery Network*', presented by none other than Latoya Jackson. There was a number on the screen you could dial to share your supernatural experiences with the host. On another channel was the live competition of Miss Teen USA.

The next morning, I met Mike, Jen's teenage son, who was sporting a Metallica T-shirt. He had a giggly voice and small eyes. He was very shy. The rest of the day I tried to catch up on my sleep. That evening, we went to Taco Bell restaurant at the harbour where Sam was working. I had never seen morbidly obese people before, let alone so many in one place.

Sam, now 21, had changed. I don't know if 'grown up' is the proper description, but he had matured. He sported weird sideburns, slick hair combed backwards, and a ponytail that rested on top of his restaurant uniform. He didn't say much as he seemed to be very immersed in his role behind the counter. Little did I know that he was just stoned.

The next evening, Sam showed up at Jen and Jake's place with his girlfriend Kacey and a friend called Ray to 'collect me'. From then on, everything was completely upside down.

My itinerary on Google Maps

The entrance to my friend's house in central Baltimore

So much has happened. I stayed in the Baltimore area for 12 days. Some days I stayed with Jake & Jen in Pikesville, and the other days with Sam in downtown Baltimore. At one point, I was locked up for two days in Sam's apartment when he was working and didn't leave me a spare key.

I got to know Sam's girlfriend and friends. Kacey was a short and attractive blonde girl, and Ray was a sporty guy with lots of wristbands. After two days at his small and slightly messy place watching them smoke lots of joints, (of which I dared not to partake) we headed to *Ocean City*. 'O.C.' is a commercial beach resort that stretches approximately 50 kilometres along the coast. It is about a three-hour's drive from Baltimore. '*Bawmore*' (as they call it) is on the *Chesapeake Bay*, and not on the coast, as I initially thought. We stayed in O.C. overnight, walking around stoned under a warm, starry sky, and drove back the next day.

I stayed at Sam's place just a couple of days, during which there was lots of smoking, and not just cigarettes or weed; the neighbour's house actually caught fire! A screaming woman was rescued by the fire department from out the window next to ours.

Due to the fire incident, I spent some time at Jake and Jen's again. As the boredom was setting in, Sam finally called asking whether I felt like coming over to his place. That's when 'it' happened. When we got to his place, he told me Kacey and Ray were missing. Naturally Sam was upset. Not much later, Kacey suddenly returned to Sam's apartment. It turned out that she and Ray had been to O.C. again – together. After a bit of shouting followed by silence, Sam told Kacey and Ray

Fire at the neighbours

to both fuck off and leave, for good. Sam told me afterwards that he had been getting annoyed with the both of them. Apparently, Ray was freeloading and he knew Kacey did not care for him as much as he did for her.

So, the world had suddenly changed for Sam. He had been planning to ask Kacey to marry him. That Thursday, he took me to an illegal rave in the middle of nowhere, partly out-doors (it was sultry hot) with really cool music and equally cool-looking people dancing. It was an amazing experience. Sam, however, felt the need to drop acid (twice in one day); and 'hunt women' on his own. It didn't feel good when his mood suddenly changed like that.

It was after that evening that I ended up getting locked up in his apartment for two days. When he finally returned, he told me he had quit his job – something I wasn't allowed to tell his dad. Soon after, he would have to leave his apartment as well.

I tried to steer clear of Sam during the rest of my stay and used my time to see the local sights. This included the University of Maryland where Jen worked, and Washington D.C. where I walked around 'The Mall', home to the White House, the US Capitol building, and several museums and embassies.

After admiring the Union Station building, I went to my Greyhound bus.

The Washington Mall

D.C. > Atlanta > New Orleans

On my way to New Orleans, via Atlanta, I met a guy named Jason. Originally from New Hampshire, he now lives and studies in 'N'Awleens'.

I figured I could trust him when he invited me over to his house. We arrived late at his place in what appeared to be a suburb of the city, with cosy-looking wooden houses. It was still extremely hot at night. There were lots of people there that I assumed were all students, except for that one girl, perhaps, who said she was smoking heroin in her cigarette. She asked where I was going and if I didn't want to travel with her instead. I politely declined.

The next morning, a car dropped me off at the French Quarter in the centre of town and getting out of the car felt like stepping into a steam-filled oven. I met an older couple, in their thirties or something, kind of straight looking, a man and a woman who said they were from Seattle. They seemed to experience New Orleans the same way I did, as the place seemed so different to them, from the climate, the smells, the food, and the language (even though it's just another accent, it was almost indecipherable to me). We hung out for a while, eating Cajun burgers in a Jazz bar that had those typical French balconies.

French Quarter, New Orleans

New Orleans > Houston > San Antonio.

In the bus from Houston to San Antonio, I met a girl called Nicole who lived in San Antonio. She gave me her phone number.

In San Antonio I stayed in a youth hostel with people from all over, including people from Turkey, Vienna, East Germany, and Switzerland. In the centre of town there was a canal with touristy venues along the water, which reminded me a bit of Utrecht back in Holland. At midnight it was hot enough for a swim. I stayed another night.

Fellow travellers

In the bus from San Antonio to El Paso, Texas,
Saturday 28 August 1993, 21:20 local time

Feeling great now. Today was my last day in San Antonio. Yesterday and today, I spent my time with Irene (Austrian) and Silke (German). I'm now walking around with the addresses or phone numbers of six people I only just met.

Travelling is great! It is so easy to make contact and experience new things. I'm getting new impressions in such a way that I have to rely more on my feelings and instincts. Feeling more alive! I had conversations that could last a lifetime, especially with Silke. Great to share our life stories in a short time and learn from each other's experiences.

In the bus from San Antonio to El Paso I was hit in the face by a black guy with a thirst buster (an oversized drinking cup) after I asked him something about the route. When I asked him what I had said wrong, he hit me again and said I should ask someone of my own 'species'. Another passenger came to my rescue and told me to avoid this crazy guy. Later I saw him talking to his drink.

I should arrive at five in the morning (this is a night journey within one state).

Wisconsin, Friday, 3 September 1993,
19:00 local time

I'm on my way to Chicago from San Francisco. Left two days ago. Met up somewhere in the middle of the Rocky Mountains with two Polish women, Ewa and Monika. Passed through Nevada and Utah earlier and had a short stop at Salt Lake City.

Stayed briefly in El Paso and walked across the border to Ciudad Juárez in Mexico. From the barbed-wire bridge over the Rio Grande you could see the low riverbank covered in graffiti with stuff written in Spanish, something about Saddam Hussein and George Bush.

The streets in Juárez were quite different; there were no skyscrapers and it smelled like a mixture of spices and garbage. The buses were really old, robust, and colourful. I walked around for a couple of hours, explored some streets outside the city centre that stretched out a long way, took some pictures, and went back via a square in the centre and some uninteresting tourist street near the border.

Juárez, Mexico

From El Paso I went to New Mexico, which my initial hosts Jake and Jen had promised would be the most beautiful place in the US (even though they hadn't been there themselves). But when I arrived in Albuquerque, it was raining, so I decided to move on. I didn't have that much time, after all, and I still had a long way to go to my final destination of New York.

Leaving Albuquerque at night, I went on to Los Angeles. Approaching the city took forever, with fields of oranges and windmills, but mostly suburbs that looked very boring ...

LA didn't seem like the kind of place to walk around, so I made a transfer to the next stop: San Francisco. The route along the Pacific Ocean had lovely scenery, reminding me of the Mediterranean coastline.

In San Fran I stayed at a youth hostel where, for the first time since travelling by bus, I washed my clothes. There were several groups of young people staying there, but I couldn't really connect with them. It was the first time I actually felt lonely and homesick. I hadn't been in touch with my family in quite a while, either. I called home, and heard the news from my mother, that my sister had given birth to a baby boy, making me an uncle for the first time. On hearing this, I no longer felt the need to talk to my mother about feeling lonely. She doesn't need to worry about me.

I walked around the hills of the city for a while, and took the famous, old-fashioned tram up the hill. From there, I enjoyed the view over the city and the bay, and could see the Golden Gate Bridge and the Alcatraz island/prison.

A long journey lies ahead.

In San Francisco, wearing my Kraftwerk T-shirt

After three days in a bus, I'm looking forward to finally being in a youth hostel again. A rest is really needed after this long journey from San Fran via the Rockies. After the Polish women left, I sat next to a very friendly big black guy on his way to Chicago. He was on his way back to his family and we chatted for a long time. At one of the stops I got out for some dinner. Peanut M&M's and a coke, which was basically my diet for most of the trip so far, apart from the odd one-dollar burger at McDonald's. I returned to the bus, and as we drove off, I ate the sweets in one go. My travel companion gave me a bit of a dirty look, apparently displeased that I didn't share any with him. I didn't want to admit to him that was basically my dinner. So, unfortunately, we didn't talk for the rest of the journey.

Arriving late in the evening at the bus station in central Chicago, I noticed the area was a bit rough. I hadn't booked a place in advance, so I had no option but to take the night bus to Detroit, ultimately one of my goals of this trip.

Quite early, around six or so, I was woken up by a guy who poked me and said something that sounded like:
'Yo bro, 'ts D'troi.'

In the central Greyhound bus station, I couldn't figure out where to leave my rucksack and asked some guy in a uniform where the baggage deposit was, but he didn't immediately understand me until he went: 'Ah, luggage!' and pointed at the walls which were lined with metal lockers.

It was early on a bright Saturday morning, and going out on the street was like entering a different world. As I did in Juárez,

Detroit skyline

I went out for a walk, trying to memorize my location for an easy return. But unlike when I was in Mexico there was hardly anyone on the street, especially the further I got from the station. I wanted to stay safe, and without another living soul walking around, or even a car out on the street, I felt fine. In the centre I walked by some empty retro-futuristic buildings. It was hard to figure out whether they were deserted permanently, or just for the weekend. Through the buildings I could see the Sci-Fi metro line, like a monorail about 10 metres high in the air, and decided to catch one. After I figured out how to get on the metro, I soon realised that not only were there no other passengers, but also no driver! I was all alone in this thing when it took off into the sky. It slowly made its way from building to building, hovering over the streets, while a robotic voice announced the stations with names like *'Cadillac Center'* and *'Times Square'*. It was like being in a film. It was a circular line, and when I thought I'd seen enough, I got out and walked by the *'Renaissance Center'*, the most modern building in the city. In front of it is a sculpture of Joe Louis' giant fist. No wonder such good soul and techno music comes from Detroit...

The buildings were all facing a big river, and Canada was on the other side. Just as I did in El Paso, I decided to walk across the border. But as Detroit is built more for cars than pedestrians, I soon realized it was going to be quite a walk. When I reached the nearest footbridge, however, an officer told me I wasn't allowed to walk across, as too many people had committed suicide by jumping off of it.

The Spirit of Detroit and the Renaissance Center

Detroit People Mover

Gershwin Hotel, New York, Tuesday,
7 September 1993, 19:00 local time.
Last (full) day.

Today I walked around in my final destination, New York. My first impression, after everything I've seen, I wasn't that impressed; more tall buildings with people just walking by each other without any contact, all in their own world.

Three days earlier, when I was in the bus from Detroit to Toronto, I had the idea to have a look around Windsor until I saw what it looked like from up close: boring suburbia. On the way to Toronto, we passed a place called London and even a River Thames – nothing like the original ones though; just more suburbia.

Toronto however was very cool. I stayed in a youth hostel in the centre where I met up with some nice people. There was a French–Swiss guy I talked to and I met a really nice girl from France who was studying in Germany and was considering moving to Canada. She was cute. I also met up with 2 girls from West Berlin and a guy from New York, who I bumped into again when I visited the CN-Tower, Canada's tallest structure.

I liked Canada, or rather Toronto, more than Ameri- ca: cleaner, safer, less racial problems while having a seemingly more (racially) diverse society. Also, the way how the streets actually have names and not numbers, and don't always seem to follow a grid pattern. Basically, it feels more European. I went to the Eaton shopping mall… unbelievable how big that is. So far, I thought San Francisco was the prettiest city I had seen so far but Toronto felt the most pleasant to be in.

On my way from Toronto to New York, I was sitting next to a Mexican girl named Veronica. She seemed quite well off, clearly not from the region I'd visited in Juarez. Despite this, she was stopped at the Niagara Falls border for a full security check; they used gloves and searched her in unpleasant places. Our initial friendly chat was muted shortly after we'd met.

Toronto's CN Tower

She said she was also going to New York and suggested we could catch up there later. I never saw her again.

I did meet some other people here in this surprisingly low priced nice hostel/hotel in the middle of Manhattan. There was a German guy from the Black Forest near Luxemburg who had done his alternative military service in a hospital. There was a Malaysian guy who was studying in London and wanted to see Europe and America. There was also one Dutch guy, who turned out to be a real dick, and a South-African guy with whom I managed to speak some Afrikaans with.

On my last night I felt tired, keen to go back home. I managed to block the toilet in the dorm room but pretended it wasn't me.

A foggy and wet New York

METROPOLIS

3

The Gift

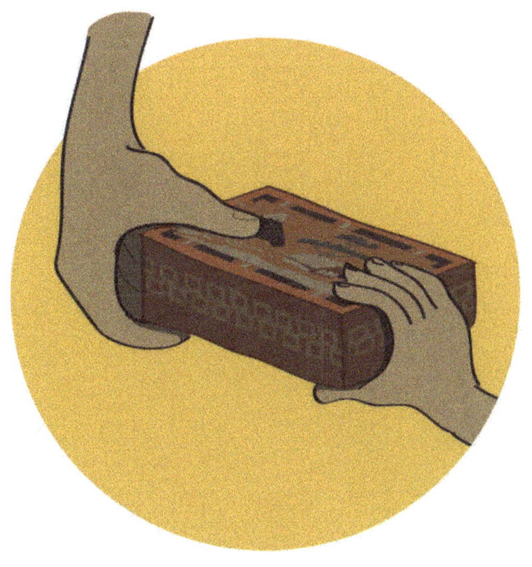

A life in colour

IT WAS PAST 9 PM
WHEN THE HERO OF
OUR STORY FOUND
HIMSELF TRYING TO
GET HOME.

THE END

73

THIS 7 YEAR OLD BOY LOVES THE SMELL OF THE WEEKLY PANCAKES.

HIS 9 YEAR OLD SISTER LOVES THEM TOO, BUT HAS DOUBTS ABOUT HER BROTHER.

THEIR MOTHER IS BAKING THE PANCAKES WHILE WAITING FOR HER HUSBAND.

HERE HE IS, DURING THEIR WEDDING 10 YEARS AGO. HE IS A PRIMARY SCHOOL TEACHER.

THIS IS HIM NOW, IN 1970. HE IS IN A HURRY, AND HE IS CARRYING SOMETHING IN HIS HANDS, HOPING TO BE HOME SOON.

STROO

ZOMP

KLK
KLK
BOOM!
?
DADDY!

AMSTERDAM, 5 YEARS LATER

I GOT THIS LITTLE BOX FROM MY FATHER WHEN I WAS YOUR AGE.

IT WILL GIVE YOU YOUR PURPOSE IN LIFE, HE SAID...

...IF YOU DO YOUR BEST IN SCHOOL....

NOW I'M GIVING IT TO YOU...!

...YOU MIGHT NEED IT ONE DAY...

...I KNOW, IT DOESN'T OPEN.

Den Haag Centraal
THE HAGUE CENTRAL STATION

5
3

QR code for soundtrack

In mathematics, an irrational number is any real number that is not a rational number – that is, it is a number which cannot be expressed as a fraction m/n, where m and n are integers, with n non-zero. Informally, this means numbers that cannot be represented as simple fractions. It can be deduced that they also cannot be represented as terminating or repeating decimals, but the idea is more profound than that. While it may seem strange at first hearing, almost all real numbers are irrational, in a sense which is defined more precisely below. Perhaps the most well known irrational numbers are π and √2.

8
2
5
4
7 3

π = 3.14159265358979323846
264338327950288419716939937
51058209749445923078164 0.....

√2 = 1.41421356237
095048801688724...
LAB

A quantum is an indivisible entity
of a quantity that is related to
both energy and momentum of
elementary particles
of matter and of
photons and..

...QUANTUMS...

?

HEY, PST! AREN'T THERE ANY GIRLS IN THIS CLASS??

HAHAHA...! GIRLS IN THEORETICAL PHYSICS CLASS... THAT'S A GOOD ONE...!

.....
SIGH.....

OKAY...WELL, THEN. THERE'S GOT TO BE A PURPOSE TO THESE CLASSES THOUGH, DON'T YOU THINK?
RESULTS

I MEAN, WHERE ARE ALL THOSE NUMBERS AND ALL GOOD FOR...? APART FROM MAKING TRAINS GO ON TIME AND ALL...?

WHAT IS THE USE OF PHYSICS IN A WORLD WITHOUT GIRLS...? WITHOUT BEAUTY? WHAT IS THE MEANING.....

...OF LIFE...?

MAN, SOUNDS LIKE YOU COULD USE ONE... YOU'RE THINKING TOO MUCH...!

?
?
THINKING... TOO MUCH...?
AT UNIVERSITY..??

???

OTJE
7

HEY...

HEY.

WHICH ONE...?
D   215
your mother called!
Call her back!

HEY... CAN I USE THE PHONE?
SURE HON...

I'LL TRY THE MOST LIKELY ONE FIRST...
THANKS

HI MOM... DAVID HERE... THOUGHT IT WOULD BE YOU... YOU RANG...?
CHEW CHEW

YES IT'S ME... I HAVE SOME SAD NEWS THOUGH....

GRANDMA HAS DIED... THIS MORNING...
KRK

WOULD YOU LIKE SOME DRY COOCKIES WITH YOUR LEMONADE LITTLE BOY...?
?
GLP
THE FUNERAL IS NEXT SATURDAY... CAN YOU COME...?

NEXT SATURDAY,
IN THE HAGUE.

NOW LET US PROCEED TO THE
RECEPTION AT MY HOUSE...
WHO IS THAT STRANGE GUY
STANDING NEXT TO MY UNCLE...?

LATER, AT MY UNCLE'S HOUSE.
DAVID, I WANT YOU TO MEET SOMEONE.

THIS IS RALF, HE IS MY STUDENT.
HE STUDIES AT THE ART SCHOOL.

SO RALF, WHAT'S IT LIKE
TO BE MY UNCLE'S PUPIL...?
PROTEGE...! YOUR UNCLE
IS A VERY GOOD PAINTER.

I CAN SHOW YOU SOME OF MY STUFF IN
HIS ATELIER...

THANKS TO YOUR UNCLE I GOT ADMITTED TO THE ART ACADEMY IN AMSTERDAM...
...BUT THESE PAINTINGS I DO ON THE SIDE...
WHAA...THEY ARE ...EHH.. BIG...!
YES, WELL...SO I HEAR YOU STUDY...PHYSICS ?

QR code for soundtrack

HOW I MET THE LOVE OF MY LIFE
AMSTERDAM,
NEW YEARS'S EVE 2003

PIZZA·SNACKS

DING
DONG

WHAT IF THIS IS AS GOOD AS IT GETS...?

I'M DROWNING HERE AND YOU ARE DESCRIBING THE WATER...!

ARE WE DONE BEING NEIGHBORS FOR NOW?
HAPPY NEWYEAR
OK GUYS, THE PARTY CAN BEGIN...!

23:59

BOOM BOOM BOOM

BOOM BOOM
!?

BOOM BOOM
HM.

OOM BOOM B
OK...

OM BOOM BO

M BOOM BOO

M'
SHE WAS MORE LIKE A
BEAUTY QUEEN FROM
A MOVIE SCENE....

WHO WILL DANCE...
ON THE FLOOR... IN THE ROUND...

BILLIE JEAN... IS NOT MY LOVER...

...SHE'S JUST A GIRL WHO CLAIMS
THAT I AM THE ONE..

Irish English Ailish

Flying over the North Sea,
16 January 2004

We met only a fortnight ago, or to be precise, our bums did, whilst dancing to *Billie Jean* on the dancefloor at a New Year's party in Amsterdam, and now I am on my way to meet her again in London.

Amsterdam, 1 January–3 January 2004

Still dark at 6:00 a.m, we spill out of the club. I manage to write down her name and number on a piece of paper with her friend's eyeliner.

She and her friends are from London. They're visiting for just a few days, and staying at a hotel in the centre of town.

The morning after the party, New Year's Day, I have a massive hangover and stay in bed. I look at the piece of paper I have in my coat pocket.

'Ailish' it says, next to a long number starting with 0044. That must be England, I think. But what is Ailish ...? Is it an adjective? An unusual name, I conclude as I call the number.

Olafur Eliasson 'The Weather Project'
The Tate Modern, London, Turbine Hall

First picture I took of Ailish on my visit.
Tate Modern.

It is Ailish indeed, an Irish name, she tells me. Her parents are Irish but she was born and raised in England. Irish English Ailish. She is out with her friends exploring the centre of Amsterdam. It is super cold, she says, but lovely. We talk about meeting up, but I am still too groggy and suggest a meetup the day after.

The next day I go to the Leidseplein and see her waiting for me. It is even colder than the day before, and it has started to snow. She has on a light blue winter coat and a woolly hat. As a native Amsterdammer, I feel like I need to take charge of the afternoon and show her around. We walk and talk a lot, but also share stretches of silence, which feels surprisingly comfortable.

The snow and cold are getting more intense, and as we pass a place called 'Gary's Muffins' on one of the canals, we decide to go inside. A flight of steps takes us down to a semi-basement full of tourists escaping the cold. It is warm inside, and we order hot tea.

Ailish talks about her friends and her impressions of Amsterdam.

'She is really nice', I think and notice that neither she – nor I – are eating anything. She says she doesn't want anything to eat, even though I think I hear her tummy rolling. I realise mine is rolling too.

We continue our walk along the canals as it gets even colder and more snow falls. Winter darkness is settling in, and as we reach a famous point where you can see five bridges in every direction, we come to a standstill. This is ridiculously romantic, I think, but I'm not sure whether I should kiss her, so I don't. I'm pretty sure she thinks the same: *Too soon …*

That evening, after hours of walking in the cold, we meet up with her friends in a café on the Utrechtsestraat. It is a typical Amsterdam-style 'brown café', or 'pub', as it is called in England she informs me. With thick red velvet curtains draped across the entrance and traditional tiny Persian rugs on the tables, it has a theatrical element to it except for the loud barman serving Heineken beer.

We order some bitterballen; typical Dutch pub snacks of the deep-fried variety, but again, neither Ailish nor I eat. Despite the protests from our stomachs, we only move the food around the bowl. Much to the amusement of her friends, our tummies have a conversation all on their own.

I enjoy telling these visitors about my birth city. They have a deep interest in Dutch culture, having been here many times before, and they clearly love the place. I feel almost proud, a feeling I am not used to. But I am also curious about where they come from, Ailish in particular. I learn that she has an interesting career as an environmental scientist, travelling the world. She has an enchanting glimmer in her eyes, as well as an overly charming and chatty tummy.

She's different, I think. She possesses a calmness that I'm not used to, and a somewhat reserved but intriguing demeanour that piques my curiosity. I like different. I have always felt different myself, partly due to being adopted, I suppose. My entire life, I have wished for a soulmate of some sort. When I was a child, I dreamt of having a twin brother or sister. As I got older, I realised that being with somebody 'just like me' wouldn't work; that would be a neurotic nightmare. My past relationships were good, but never quite 'right'. But now my instincts are telling me something new. This is something. Something special. Someone special.

As the evening comes to an end I head back home, but not before agreeing to meet up with Ailish again the next day.

I have lived in Amsterdam on and off for over 15 years and believe I know every square inch of it. But now, through the eyes of these visitors, it seems new to me. Through Ailish's eyes. Coincidentally, their hotel is next to the house I had lived in when I was around four years old, close to the old Heineken brewery. And it is here, on the corner of the square I know so well, after yet another few hours of walking and talking our way around Amsterdam, that we have our first kiss. The cold doesn't bother us in the slightest, in fact, it emphasises our warmth.

There is only one day left before Ailish and her friends will return to London; one more day of walking around in the cold, not eating, and kissing. That day lasts forever and goes by in a split second.

The time has come to say goodbye, and we leave it at an 'until we meet again' sentiment. She gives me her address, which is in Islington, a place in North London I have never heard of. She lives there with five other people including the house owners, kind of like a student house for adults. Typically London, apparently. I am hooked and accept her invitation to visit her in the very near future.

So here I am, two weeks later. I just landed at Stansted Airport on a ridiculously cheap low budget airline. The train takes me straight into Liverpool Street Station and central London to meet Ailish.

I notice how busy and crowded the station is, and suddenly realise that we didn't agree on an exact meeting point. It's so energetic and loud, so many different kinds of people all sharing this busy place.

And all of a sudden, at just five foot one, Ailish stands out tall from the crowd, dispersing people, like Moses opening up the Red Sea. I see her smiling at me, and from that moment on, I know all will be good.

37 Mornington Cres

More London photos online

4

From Poland to Holland

Time immemorial
A family discovery

The stranger in me

In Haarlem, a small city near Amsterdam where I live, I often feel like an outsider. I've felt like an outsider most of my life.

In Haarlem I am a Londoner.
In London I was an Amsterdammer.

In Amsterdam I spoke like I was from The Hague.
In The Hague I was the born Amsterdammer.

In England I was the Dutchie.
In Holland I talk and think in English.

At university I was the creative type.
At art school I was 'that serious guy'.

At my high school I was from a lower class.
At work as a designer I feel too cerebral.

When in the company of Christians I am an atheist.
When in the company of atheists I am a Jew.

When with left-wingers I am a conservative,
When with right-wingers I am an artist.

When I am with the family I grew up with I am
    a complicated thinker.
When I am with my biological family I am
    a relaxed guy that wants to laugh.

When I am with my brother I am small.
When I am with my sister I am tall.

So who the hell am I?

The Mystery of The Name

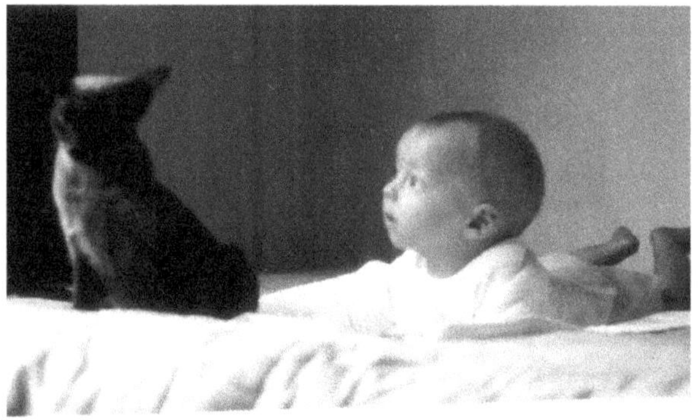

This is me. The Siamese next to me is called Gunja. I still like cats.

My first name is *David*, pronounced 'Da veet', the Hebrew way, as both my mothers insist – my 'biological' mother as well as my 'adoptive' mother. I was born in Amsterdam and brought back to the *Onbekende Gracht* (the Unknown Canal in English) – where my 22-year-old birth mother was living at the time.

I am just a few months old in this picture and it might well have been taken on the day I was adopted, in the summer of 1970. Adopted, just like Moses, Superman, Batman, Spiderman and Steve Jobs. So I'm in good company.

The story goes that when I was introduced to my new home and wider family members in The Hague, my new grandfather, an artist, gave a quick assessment of me after seeing my little worried face: 'He will either be a poet or a philosopher,' he said.

I'm not sure if he knew it at the time, but my second given name is *Dylan*, after the then popular Welsh poet Dylan Thomas, and a rebellious Jewish folk singer with an intrusive voice, better known as Bob Dylan.

As a child growing up in Holland, none of these people were of interest to me, although I thought the name 'Dillen' sounded cool.

My third name, *Jona* (Dutch spelling of Jonah) – meaning 'dove' in Hebrew – has invoked the imagination of many because of the guy in the belly of the whale story. The poor man had the task of delivering a message of mischief, and who wants to listen to bad news …?

As I was never officially adopted, I kept my birth mother's last name, *Enker*. It may sound like a Dutch name, but it isn't.

For a long time, I thought I was the only Enker in the world, apart from my cousin in Belgium.

Then in the mid-nineties, I came across a book called *In Memoriam*, listing all the Jews deported from the Netherlands during the Holocaust. I knew my grandfather had fled Germany to Holland and survived the war. Of course, he himself was not on the In Memoriam list, but his parents, my great grandparents, were.

The rest of my relatives are from Poland. Other relatives had already escaped pre-war Poland to live in America and Israel.

Most of my family was a big mystery to me but unusually for many who are adopted, I had some clues. It turned out there was a lot more to the name, to the family, and to my identity than I could have imagined.

ENKER (F) - Enker also appears in the form Anker which is the German word for "anchor". The anchor was a symbol of hope and salvation and was often used as a good luck sign on homes and business establishments. It was selected as a family name for that reason.

From the book of Jewish surnames

David Enker was born in Grojec, Poland in 1883. He was a merchant and married. David was murdered in the Shoah.

From Yad Vashem

Carved in stone: detail of the national monument
for the Holocaust victims in Amsterdam

Life is
a gift.

Don't take
it for
granted.

115

LONDON

5

From London to Tel Aviv

2004–2011
London

Tower Bridge, Southbank

Milennium Bridge, St Paul's Cathedral

Milennium Bridge, Tate Modern

Hot Munchies, under the bridge

Avi & Zaina

It was not long after the Israel-Lebanon war in 2006 that I met Avi. I was working in London at a famous ad agency in Knightsbridge, between Hyde Park and Harrods, nicknamed 'the banner factory'.

I was already there for half a year as a freelance designer by the time Avi arrived.

The 7th of July, 2006 was the first anniversary of the 7/7 bombings. Exactly one year ago I was on the Piccadilly Line metro on my way to Richmond, between Kings Cross and Russell Square when a terrorist blew himself up, killing 26 people and wounding and traumatising several hundreds more, including me.

To commemorate, I left home a bit earlier that day so I could be on the Piccadilly Line, between those same two stations again, without being blown to pieces, as a way of saying: *I am alive, you bastards!*

When I arrived at work I was expecting that at least some people would be talking about it, but no one did. Perhaps work is not the best place to discuss these things, I thought, but then, many more sensitive things get discussed, at least by a few outspoken colleagues. Someone mentioned it briefly, but I didn't want a pity party or anything;

so, I never mentioned my experience to any colleague there. It didn't feel like the right place to mention such a thing.

I got stuck at this company for a while. The work was utterly stupid and pointless, but it was a stop gap for me. Luckily, there were a few people I got along with. One guy, Paul, often played James Brown and Kraftwerk loudly. There was also a healthy number of females to balance out the otherwise nerdy male environment.

Around this time, Lebanon was launching rockets into Israel on a regular basis. Not long after, in order to stop the bombardment, Israel retaliated, going after Hezbollah and bombing several places in Lebanon.

It just so happened that one of the women at work had a Lebanese background. Her name was Zaina. She said that her mother was Lebanese and her father was French. She grew up in France and spoke French and Arabic. Apart from this, she was a typical Londoner, following (or setting) the latest fashion trends, going out on the town, and laughing a lot. She wore a tiger-skinned scarf (or sometimes one of those 'in support of Palestine' scarves). She and Paul were friends and shared an interest in quoting articles from *The Guardian* out loud about art and design, but also politics. 'Stupid Bush this' and 'stupid Bush that'; that sort of commentary. The more anti-capitalist, the better. Ironic really, while working for one of the biggest commercial advertising agencies in the world.

The conflict between Israel and Lebanon grew as did the tension in the office. One day, I was sitting next to Zaina, when she turned to me and said: 'You know, I can understand that people blow themselves up (in order to kill Israelis)'.

I'm not sure why she said this to me. Did she assume I would 'like' this statement – that I am 'naturally' on her side or something?

I didn't mention that I narrowly missed being killed by a suicide bomber just the year before.

Nor did I mention that my German-born Jewish grandfather barely escaped the Nazis, but his parents didn't and were gassed in Auschwitz, not far from the area in Poland where they were born and chased away from, and that there is a country for people like them to be safe from persecution, the place where they originate from, called Israel.

All I could utter were some vague nuances, some grey question marks regarding violence and peace. Offended by my apparent lack of support she got up and left in tears.

From then on, certain subjects were avoided in the office, in my presence at least.

I didn't often join the office social events, which mostly involved 'getting wasted'.

To most of the English colleagues I was just a quiet version of *Goldmember*, their only reference to a Dutch person (or incarnation of one, thanks to Austin Powers).

Shortly after this mini drama, Avi joined the company, as a developer. Like Zaina, he had olive skin, black hair and dark eyes. On the first Friday pub outing, I decided to join in and found myself talking with him.

At first, I couldn't tell where he was from, as he wasn't saying much, and when he did, he behaved in a loud, jovial way, which made me think he was Italian or something.

'I am from the Holy Land', he said with a broad smile with lots of teeth. After a very brief pause he continued: '… from Israel, haha!'

When I told him my mother lived there as a child, his eyes lit up. He told me his dad was English, and that he briefly lived in Jersey with some relatives before he moved to London, initially working in falafel joints before somehow ending up in the banner factory.

After that, we started chatting, and like a Woody Allen movie, the background scenery kept on changing but the conversation just carried on.

I was living near Swiss Cottage at the time while Avi was just a bit further north in Golders Green, known for its many Jewish and Japanese residents. He had a Japanese girlfriend. By the time we got to know each other a bit more, it was approaching winter, and it was getting colder and wetter outside, but that didn't stop us from continuing our conversations, at work or along the Finchley Road where our bus stopped every day. The storm between Israel and Lebanon had also calmed down at this point; however, I noticed that Zaina never talked to Avi directly. Instead, she just conversed in 'general terms', and completely omitted her political rants in his, or my, presence.

Avi told me that he had completed part of his military service in Lebanon, but otherwise he didn't have much to say about his life in Israel. Zaina didn't know this, but the fact that he was Israeli was clearly alarming for her. She didn't seem able to place this odd and jolly guy into her version of what an Israeli was.

In contrast, Avi didn't care that Zaina was Lebanese and made friendly attempts to approach her. But she would brush him off and slink off to her fan club.

Finally, there was a shake-up in upper management that caused most of us to leave the company, and Avi and I moved on at the same time, even having a joint goodbye party.

Witnessing this tension between my former co-workers, as well as knowing my own connection to Israel aroused my curiosity about the country. So many conflicting opinions about one place. Clearly there must be something special about it I thought, something really special.

Crystal Palace, London

Hampstead

Tulse Hill

Baker Street Tube Station (the world's oldest)

QR code for soundtrack

The Holy Land

It was before sunrise on the 2nd of May 2008 when Ailish and I flew over the city of Tel Aviv. I was deeply excited to see the country that I had heard so much about, the country to which I felt a strange attraction and connection: similar yet different, eastern yet western, ancient yet modern, secular yet Jewish. Just like my ancestors. Would the people be like me?

It was just about to get light when we landed at Ben Gurion Airport. Out of the plane, touching the tarmac, I thought of kissing the ground, but realised the idiocy of this idea. The sultry smell and blue light felt Mediterranean, but unlike Spain or Italy – it was different. This is the *Levant*, the birthplace of Jews and Jesus.

On this trip I had no intention of getting caught up in the 'Messiah Syndrome', a phenomenon in which one is convinced that they are a holy figure upon visiting the Holy Land – but would I be able to resist being absorbed into this homeland for Jews in some other way? According to Israeli Law, you only need one Jewish grandparent to 'make Aliyah', that is, to migrate and become an Israeli citizen. Through some weird loophole it turns out that I have that link; my maternal grandfather Max was a Jew, born in Germany. I only briefly met him when I was a child, during the time I lived with my adoptive family. So, there is a thread to Jewish roots.

When my mother, his daughter, was a teenager, the family moved to Israel. My grandfather was some kind of figure in the international Hebrew-Christian alliance, but that wasn't a profession much liked in the nascent Jewish state. After a few years, the family returned to Holland, and when the turbulent relationship with my grandmother (Oma Z) finally ended, he returned to the 'faith of his forefathers'. And here I was, in the land of his forefathers.

My friend Avi and his girlfriend Aiko were supposed to pick us up at the airport, but they hadn't arrived yet. (Since our time in London working together, Avi had thrown in the towel and returned home.)

It was safe to say that most people that were in the plane and now in the airport were Jews. Some were religiously dressed, but most people were like anyone else; regular, seemingly secular people, families, businessmen, yet all with a background not unlike mine: a history of being part of a minority; mostly persecuted, whose ancestors fled from eastern European countries to reach the west. Even the Mizrachi – Jews from Arab countries who make up the majority of Israeli Jews – escaped their birth lands.

Is it possible that the trauma of persecution was inherited and innate in my birth mother's state of being? Did it play a role in her giving me away as a baby? There is no doubt my birth mother was, and is, traumatised. She and her siblings are all recognised as second generation war victims. Even now, she can't stop talking about the war, her father, and Judaism.

My birth mother's link to Israel is through family history. As for me, that line is broken. Instead, I hope to feel a connection on a different level: genetics, looks, instincts, basal stuff, like a long-lost sibling or something.

Avi and Aiko entered the airport, all smiles. After a warm welcome we went outside and climbed into Avi's father's car. Excited to see each other and to explore this new place, we sped off.

On the motorway, the green and yellow ochre landscape passed by our window.

'So, this is Israel', I thought, bending slightly forward to get a better look from the backseat.

Just at that moment, a police car behind us with its siren on came closer. 'Oh-oh …', Avi murmured, '… we need to pull over …'

'For what?' I was thinking, '… a faulty indicator light or something..? Or maybe something more serious; are they looking for drugs … or terrorists …?'

Avi nonchalantly got out of the car and started talking to the officer. I could hear him laughing, seemingly charming his way out of the situation. He got back in the car, slammed the door, and said: 'You need to put on your seatbelts.' He laughed again. 'We got off with a warning, ha-ha …!'

Avi was living in a city called *Rehovot*, as average an Israeli city as it gets. He rented an apartment on the 10th floor in the centre of town. The lift in the building was 'Shabbat proof' meaning that it worked by itself, whether anyone was along for the ride or not. Any form of 'work' is prohibited during Shabbat, and operating a lift is considered 'working'. The lift spends its merry day stopping at every floor, just in case. I realised religiosity and secularism go hand in hand in this country. For me, as somebody who once called himself a staunch atheist but gradually grew more open to religious sensitivities, this is an odd but interesting example of understanding both sides of the religious divide.

Jerusalem

Tel Aviv

Rehovot

Sea of Galilee

Hamat Gader

Negev Desert

Haifa

City of David
Wailing Wall

After midnight cafe in TA

Dead Sea

Neve Tzedek, TA

Zion Square, JLM

Street sign in Rehovot
רח' יבנה
ش. يفنه
REHOV YAVNEH

As we walked around town, we followed street signs in Hebrew, Arabic, and English. The people around us were generally youthful, busy, and diverse in their style and ethnicity. Many appeared to have Ethiopian heritage. Avi himself is partly Yemeni, partly English, and therefore typical for an Israeli, having some mixed background. There was an exciting buzz in the air, as if everybody was celebrating life and the fact that they were safe and free to express their Jewish identity.

Am I Jewish? According to Orthodox Jewish law I am not, as your mother needs to be Jewish, and only my mother's father was, so she would be called a 'father-Jew', which is not accepted by the orthodoxy. In America, however, with my name and background I would easily pass as Jewish. I could even apply for Israeli citizenship based on my one Jewish grandparent. Bizarrely, this was also a rule used by the Nazis to help them efficiently exterminate anyone with Jewish ancestry. Genetically I am indeed 25% Ashkenazi Jewish, as a DNA test showed. A *Quarter Jew*.

Ultimately, what counts is how I feel myself, and I cannot deny that I felt a kinship with these people on the street before me, their expressive, hurried love for life, their awkwardness and constantly being misunderstood.

I found myself wondering, if after living a comparatively individualistic existence, could I live in a country where everyone is defined by its shared past…?

Israel is roughly divided into four parts: The secular West, with Tel Aviv and surroundings, the more religious East, with Jerusalem and the Dead Sea, the tranquil North, with the Sea of Galilee, and the wild South, with the Negev desert.

Ailish and I visited all these places. While in Jerusalem, I was putting a prayer written on a piece of paper into a crack in the Western Wall (locally known as the Kotel), when I was interrupted by a hack rabbi trying to sell me something; not exactly the spiritual moment I was hoping for. We stayed in the secular, somewhat posh neighbourhood of Rehavia in Jerusalem, from where we visited the Old City, as well as Zion Square, the centre of the 'western' part of the city, where we witnessed Orthodox Jews dancing to techno music.

We went to the Sea of Galilee (locally known as The Kinneret), where we dipped our toes in the same water Jesus walked on, enjoying the tranquillity before the next shipment of tourists arrived. We went to Solomon's Mines in the middle of the Negev desert with a Jeep, driven by Ailish, and down to the most southern tip to the beach resort of Eilat, a small, ugly tourist spot overrun by thrill-seeking Russians. We passed along the Dead Sea, the lowest point on Earth, and one of the most serene places I have ever seen.

I love this land. And even though I could move there if I wanted to, I feel like I'm best off where I am now, in Haarlem, where I can also be who I want to be. As my mother always says: 'Wherever you go, you will always bring yourself.'

Bakkumstraat, Haarlem

6

From Haarlem
to Mars

2011–onward
Post-London life

WAKING
HOURS

It's 5AM and a burning sensation drives me out of bed. A toilet visit is required as my bladder is about to burst. Perhaps I shouldn't have had that big cup of herbal tea before going to bed, even though it's what helps me get to sleep in the first place ...

After a long pee I don't go back to bed. Ailish is in a deep and much needed sleep and I don't want to disturb her with my tossing and turning, complaining, sweating and moaning, so I decide to go to the back room overlooking the neighbours' gardens.

It is pitch black outside. Everyone is still asleep. There is no moon visible because of the clouds, or it is just simply not there. It is extremely quiet.

I walk downstairs to the living room, greeted by two yawning, surprised looking cats.

'That early already?' they miaow, and rub their whiskers against my leg. After I've fed them I fetch a bowl of cereal and a tea. Out front, it is just as quiet as at the back, albeit somewhat lighter with the street lights, so I keep the curtains closed.

I realise there is no point going back to bed. I get out my notebook and pen and start to write. I've been having these early wake-ups for years now, and writing gives me a feeling of control, or at least the illusion of it; it also soothes my anxiety and depression, and makes me feel better. The creative juices flow in the early hours, and the mind comes up with more material.

So let's talk about croissants …

The Amazing Croissant

Nothing like the smell of fresh coffee and the sound of hissing coffee machines. Outside it is a cold, wet and grey Tuesday in January. Inside it is warm. I enter the café in the hope of getting some work done in relative peace and quiet. The staff are milling around, still setting up the place.

I am not the first customer, as someone just leaves when I arrive. Once seated, I realize this is a brief moment of silence. This place is frequented by kids from the nearby school, and is sometimes full of seventeen-year-old girls pretending to be adults with coffee just before class.

The people working here are friendly but also somewhat awkward. The place has only been open for a couple of months now and it still has a strange feel to it. It's all shiny and clean and seemingly organised, but when I ask for a croissant with my cappuccino, things start to get a little messy.

The woman tells me it might take a while because the croissant needs to be heated. It didn't even occur to me that I don't actually like it warm, let alone hot, and to ask for a cold one. Yet the woman is still concerned about the thing being warmed and asks if I like it with jam or cheese or both. After I tell her I'm fine without anything on it she asks worriedly if I'm sure, not even with butter?

A couple of minutes later she gets back to me and asks: "not even with some cheese…?"
I smile and say that plain will really do fine.

Once I received the cappuccino the woman is gone. Is she personally overseeing the croissant working place..?

A young girl – her daughter? – comes from the back. No croissant.

What is happening with my croissant?

The woman is back now but still no sign of my croissant. I dip the little bitter cookie in my cappuccino and after the first sip the girl comes and delivers my croissant on a big plate.
"Here you are sir, your warm croissant. Would

you like something with that, some butter or
cheese or jam perhaps?"
I reply that plain will really do fine with the
broadest smile possible.

Once finished I put the empty plate at the side
of the table. A couple of minutes later the
girl comes to my table and takes the plate. She
asks if it was nice with an inquiring smile. I
wanted to say it was the best croissant I ever
had in my life, but instead, I politely smile
back and say yes, it was nice, thank you.

The bill arrives, and comes to €5,40. I
have a 5 euro bill I hand over, and then get
into this dilemma. I'm still not really sure
how and if tipping works in Holland, having
lived in the UK for 7 years where they do tip.
Ideally I would have a €1 coin that will cover
a tip as well, but I don't have one. Instead,
I have a €2 coin and a 50 ct. coin. If I give
the 50 ct. coin it might be considered an
insult with 10 ct. tip, but if I give the €2
coin it might be too much in the case that
tipping is not done here. Slightly panicked,
I give the 50ct. coin. I'm not sure if I need
to wait for the 10ct. return but the girl is
quick enough to say thank you very much while
throwing 10 cents from the till in a tip
cup while I'm awkwardly putting on my jacket
– again.

As I walk out I already feel guilty,
thinking I should have given the €2 coin for
this amazing croissant adventure.

Looking for somewhere else to work, I
already have one foot in another cafe down the

street when I remember I don't actually like the place because of its formulaic service, like a supermarket. Uttering 'shit!' just a bit too loudly, I leave and close the door behind me.

I see a woman laughing at me through the glass door. Although the place has nice juices and bagels, I realise I prefer awkward after all.

'That's a start,' I think, and close my notebook. Feeling lighter, I prepare the breakfast as the alarm sounds upstairs.

(Advertisement)

Yom Kippur on Mars

Since moving to Holland from the UK and subsequently moving house twice after that, Ailish and I really needed a sunny holiday. Having previously enjoyed the Greek islands of Lefkas and Samos, we decided to go to Greece again, this time exploring the larger island of Lesbos.

The island seemed to give credit to its name, seeing as we arrived at the tail end of a major 'women's festival'. Lesbos reminds me of Mars in the film, Total Recall, from its rough, dry, red and rugged soil and mountains, to the fact that it's a 20 million year old volcano. With the KKE (The Greek Communist Party) graffiti scattered all over the island, it could easily be the hideout for the *Martian Resistance Front*. Some people indeed looked like they could have been characters from that film with their leathery skin aided by an over-abundance of sun, feta and olive oil, and the Mediterranean pace of life.

Perfect conditions for a good read though. I finished Michel Houellebecq's *The Map and the Territory*, and read quite a bit of Chaim Potok's *The Gift of Asher Lev*. On the side I read *Collapse: How Societies Choose to Fail or Succeed*, by Jared Diamond. Excellent reads, each in their own way. And time passed by just like that.

Yom Kippur, the day of atonement, fell within the days of our stay in Lesbos. In recent years I have tried to fast on that day. However, fasting under such hot and dry conditions was perhaps not such a great idea. Best to give it a pass this time.

Ailish and I decided to spend our last day there relaxing on the beach. After our last delicious breakfast we were among the very few on the beach. I was already lobster-like, so decided to avoid the sun for a while, and sat in the shadow of a tree. Slowly, something didn't feel right, so I requested an early hotel return. We had to leave very early the next day, so I had to feel fit to fly. But I didn't feel fit at all.

It came quickly. Sweat. Fever. Vomit. Diarrhea. Cooling down. Heating up. Sweat again. More vomit. More diarrhea. Again. And again. And again.

Ailish managed to get a doctor to come to our hotel. This doctor had just finished a shift at the 24-hour service centre and wasn't supposed to be working. She was very friendly, nevertheless, and set up an I.V. in my arm, to give me a saline infusion. She also gave me an anti-sickness shot in my right butt cheek, which indeed helped a bit. The idea was to get me well, in time for our early morning flight. At least we got another chance to talk a bit more with a local. We learned that the doctor was 27 years old and wanted to leave Lesbos to follow her friends to Berlin where they apparently had better prospects.

After my mini Greek tragedy I tried to sleep, but the next morning the sickness still hadn't left me. So we had no choice but to cancel our flight. Then we found out it was the last flight of the season.

More help was required. A health clinic about 22 kilometres away was ready to take me in that day for a more thorough treatment. Once I was able to stand up, which was around three o'clock in the afternoon, Ailish drove us to the village up in the mountains. Another infusion and jab in the butt was followed by some blood tests.

Another young doctor helped me, who had already been awake for a day and a half. She must have put the needle in my hand the wrong way, because hours and hours passed, yet the bottle of saline fluid remained full. A nurse ultimately came to the rescue, and after a bit of painful fiddling, the liquid started to enter my veins at a considerably fast pace, resulting in a swollen hand. More than six hours later, I was finally discharged, and we went back to the hotel.

The next day we managed to get our return trip and all other extra costs sorted through our travel insurance, which was good news, but we still had to figure out how to get back home.

Two days after our first attempt, we tried to leave again. We managed to get to the airport at the other side of the island, which was a two-hour's drive. We were able to catch a domestic flight to Athens on one of those smaller planes with propellers at the side. We arrived in Athens in less than an hour, without any issues . But by then, I was actually starting to feel delirious; the endorphins must have started to kick in.

The first part of the four-hour wait at the airport was all right, but once we were at the gate, I started to feel anxious, panicky even. On the second flight, I sat next to a large, sweaty, beer drinking, very grumpy Dutch guy. I felt trapped and was close to running back out of the plane to lie down on the tarmac for a sleep, or a poo, or both.

Luckily, I managed to control myself and after spending the second half of the 3,5-hour trip in a meditative-like state, I felt like the worst part was over; we were nearly home.

So, I spent Yom Kippur fasting after all, albeit with a slight delay.

(Advertisement)

7

Getting Out There

2012
Haarlem

Swimming pool "De Houtvaart"

Houtmanpad

Grote Markt

Lepelstraat, Haarlem

Oude Groenmarkt, Haarlem

The Leidsebuurt
Neighbourhood in Haarlem

Rambam in the Sauna

Friday morning at the local gym. After about a half an hour of moving weights around, I was ready to leave. But first, the sauna.

I prefer to be alone in the sauna if possible, but when I opened the door I could see two large, bald, naked men through the mist. I manoeuvred past them, mumbling something about 'getting myself to the high bench'. One man simply grunted but the other one was a bit more outspoken and said 'that's fine,' as I passed. They did what most men do there; sit on their towels so their business hangs out on full display, even in a mixed-gender sauna. Not the most pleasant view. I kept my towel covering my waist, like a Roman.

We sat in silence for a while. Then one of the members of the large, bald, and naked community got up and left.

I was still sitting on the high bench that didn't have a foot-rest, so my feet were dangling quite close to the hot coals, but not so close as to be burnt . The guy noticed this, however, and said I should sit somewhere else so I wouldn't burn my feet.

'It's fine,' I said as I felt quite comfortable with my arms spread wide over the edge of the wooden bench behind me.

He then said something about fires and sacrifices and ancient gods.

I didn't understand what he meant; was he saying I shouldn't put my feet in the coal in order not to displease the gods or something …?

He was incredibly bald, and like his head, his entire body was shiny and hairless, and he had a number of tattoos. Now and then he would wipe the sweat off his arms and legs and it would land on me.

He continued to talk about his ancient gods, and then, ironically, went on about hygiene.

Jokingly, I said that hygiene and religion are an unusual combination of topics, though I have no idea why I said that.

In the loudness of his laughter, I detected a certain antipathy toward me, which was unnerving.

He then said something about rabbis, which I didn't understand. I started to wonder what direction this conversation was going in. Was he some sort of anti-Semite? Or just anti-religious in general? Or was I just being paranoid? Either way, I became more curious and feigned ignorance.

He mentioned Alexander the Great, how he was promised a great empire by The Oracle if he would untie the complicated *Gordian Knot*, which he did by just slicing it with his sword.

I told Big Baldy I thought this was a great story, speaking to the imagination.

Except that this was real, he replied, Alexander did have the greatest empire ever.

I told him it reminded me of the mythical King Arthur, with the sword and all, except that Camelot was not nearly as big as Alexander's empire.

I still wasn't sure what Mr Naked was trying to say though. Perhaps that oracles are bogus or that storytellers use too much imagination or something …

Then came a succession of information that surprised me; he had read about people who were able to trace their Jewish heritage back to before the Inquisition of 1492 and the expulsion from Spain, and who could now reclaim Spanish citizenship. Naked Dude went on to mention Maimonides, who under Moorish occupation chose to convert from Judaism to Islam.

Maimonides, or Rabbi Moses ben Maimon, also known as *The Rambam*, was a 12th century Jewish philosopher whose portrait I saw in the Chabad house in North London a couple of years back … I remember reading a bit about him, that he was also a doctor and travelled via North Africa to the Holy Land, a rare move at the time.

I told Naked Man that Maimonides feigned his conversion and ultimately chose to be Jewish again.

He mumbled a bit. I was really surprised by this man's knowledge of all this Jewish stuff but couldn't really place it.

He then mentioned he had a schoolteacher when he was a child who apparently had Spanish-Jewish ancestors because she had a name with an 'x' in it that had to be pronounced differently. Somehow this anecdote of his seemed to indicate this was the only encounter he had actually ever had with a Jew. I told him my grandfather was a Jew and had to flee

Germany because of the Nazis and that it wasn't a choice.

He went silent again before saying that I could claim German citizenship. He mentioned something about other Jews that could easily claim German heritage, especially with the thorough German bureaucracy.

I still wasn't sure if he wanted to be polite after my 'revelation' or if he was perhaps a Jew himself, albeit a rather lonely one, or just some bald naked guy with too much time and obsessions on his hands with an above-average interest in history and religion.

He thanked me for getting through the 15 minutes that he had set the sandglass for, wished me a nice day, and left the cabin.

'Likewise' I said, and stayed behind a bit.

(Advertisement)

Silence

The Haarlem Jewish Monument

Today is Memorial Day for the victims of the Second World War. This commemoration is held every year in Holland, on the 4th of May.

I realised I hadn't actually participated in the past, not with other people anyway, apart from maybe looking out of the window at 8:00 p.m. to see if people on the street were standing still for two minutes. (Two minutes of silence are kept at 8:00 p.m. nationwide each year to acknowledge those who lost their lives during the Second World War.)

So this year, Ailish and I decide to go to the memorial site in the centre of town dedicated to the seven hundred Jews taken from Haarlem. The memorial was only recently established, despite the events having taken place decades ago. Strangely enough, the memorial is hidden away on a little back street, next to a car park and some underground bin deposit containers. You really have to look for the place or know where to find it.

But perhaps that is only fitting, since it is placed right where the Jewish neighbourhood, synagogue, and rabbi's house were located all those years ago. The synagogue doesn't exist anymore and has been replaced by a modern cinema. The old canal house where the rabbi used to live is still there, but it is just a regular house now.

Like in so many other places in Holland, Jewish life was wiped out; people were deported and murdered, and synagogues destroyed. So the many picturesque places take on a different meaning if you know what happened there not so long ago. Thus, it is perhaps good that you have to put in a little effort in order to find this spot, which like the truth, often hides behind a mask.

I don't have a personal connection with this place, but I do have a personal connection with the Holocaust. My Jewish great-grandparents were murdered in Auschwitz, and their son, my grandfather, who, despite having survived Westerbork and Theresienstadt camps, had to live with the memory of seeing his parents being taken away while he was left behind. This is the kind of knowledge where words become meaningless and the pain is so great that it creates an emotional vacuum that permeates through generations. Finding a goal in life becomes a quest for meaning and goodness. Things might look rosy, beautiful, and friendly, but they can turn ugly at any moment.

Today is such a beautiful day, with a calm evening sun, the sound of seagulls and the smell of spring, as we pass the beautiful, large square around the church via the modern cinema towards the memorial. I read that wearing a kippah was desired for the occasion, but since I don't have one, I feel a bit self-conscious. But on approaching the site through an alley, I see that many of the men aren't wearing one and I feel somewhat relieved. Out of the corner of my eye, I spot the only religious figure: the current local rabbi. He seems relatively young, perhaps 40 or so.

He explains that there is no appointed leader for the occasion and also no rules. He then asks the crowd to move a little closer as he is about to give a proper speech. His voice is solemn, and in a melodic manner he reads out the names of the concentration camps to which these local Jews had been deported and murdered.

I can't stop thinking that it is somewhat painful that these people have to be commemorated by the names of the places where they were murdered, not the places where they had lived and might have known joy and love. There is the occasional Hebrew mixed in with the Dutch, including some Psalms by King David, of which I can understand a word or two, and feel a little more connected.

During his speech, just before eight o'clock, a pizza delivery guy passes behind us on a scooter, its sound echoing around the otherwise quiet place, but everybody seems determined not to be distracted, apart from one or two tutting glances. Suddenly the church bells of several nearby churches start their prelude to the two-minute silence, and the rabbi stops talking.

.

.

.

.

.

.

.

.

.

.

.

The entire place is mute. And not just us, the rabbi, and the other bystanders; as far as the ears can detect, in the rest of the city, there is not a single sound: not a cough, nor sneeze, not even breathing. As if time stands still – a single short moment that lasts forever.

The eight o'clock sun casts a warm yellow-orange light over the top halves of the old, red-stoned façades of the centuries-old houses, just visible behind the black marble memorial stones bearing the names of the deceased.

A few seagulls fly overhead, cawing as if they are mocking us, but they are simply living in the moment, a reminder that despite all the tragedies, life goes on.

The Rothko Light

Art isn't about what you see. What did I know...?

It was somewhere in the second half of the nineties that I got accepted at the *Rietveld Art Academy,* one of, if not *the* most prestigious art school in the Netherlands, somewhat comparable in style to Goldsmith's in London. I was accepted after displaying some of my oil paintings and a folio of my photographs neatly glued on black paper. My artwork was sort of surreal and melancholic, perhaps representing my mood at the time. I had previously ended my university career in physics, having realized that interested as I was in theoretical science, infinite numbers and Einstein's theories,

I didn't see myself having an actual career in it, wearing a white coat and spending my days in the laboratory.

Growing up with my strange, mixed background, I never knew what I wanted to be, or 'who to become' and all that. Part of my background is coloured by artists in the family and so I gave in to deeper yearnings in my subconscious and started drawing and painting.

The initial pride and joy of being admitted at the Rietveld soon got brushed over by the very nature of the school itself and its students. This was a place where drunken teachers, too keen on young students, applaud the junkies, prostitutes, and disruptors for creating a 'tampon in a tea-cup' and calling it art.

On one occasion, we had to make an etching, and after I tried my best to make an image of a closed eye, one teacher exclaimed 'Ah, a cunt. Finally you're getting loose'.

Halfway through the term, I visited the *Stedelijk Museum of Modern Art*. With modern art, you always have to look for references and associations, otherwise you just see a bunch of strokes on a canvas. In my case, I was already familiar with the impressionists and the surrealists, somewhat resembling the paintings by my family. There is always Monet, Renoir, and Van Gogh of course, and the sweet and melancholic early work of Picasso before he got all cocky. Then there is the beautifully mysterious work of Giorgio de Chirico preceding the surrealist work of Dali, and the humorously paradoxical work of Magritte.

But I had seen most of them before, and nice as they were, I was looking for something new. This sort of postmodern stuff from the found objects of Marcel Duchamp and the other 'hero' at the Rietveld, the installations and performances by Josef Beuys, and similar stuff after that, never really did it for me. By just having an 'idea', and then poorly executing it – or not – the 'artist' becomes an overly cerebral, soulless and arrogant ego-tripper. Life is difficult enough than to be wasted by 'pranksters'.

So, as I was wandering through the rooms of the Stedelijk Museum, running almost, ticking the points of references and annoyances, dodging the other visitors, I found myself in a room that I hadn't been in before. Usually when I am in a museum and enter a room, I scan the contents, and within a second I can tell whether it will be worth it to investigate further or move along. At first glance, I noticed that this particular room had some abstract work. Within a fraction of a second my eyes flew over the artwork and came to an abrupt halt on one painting.

Even if you haven't experienced it first-hand, everybody knows the concept of love at first sight. It's when words become suddenly pointless. Sort of like trying to explain a joke. Words, just like any other medium, deserve their own place. Certain feelings and emotions can only be expressed in one way, and more often than not it remains to be seen if a connection takes place at all. You might know that feeling when you hear a song, and it is almost as if that person made it just for you, and you alone, even though that person died before you were born. From one soul to the next. It almost becomes annoying when you find out that other people also like that same song, but for a totally different reason. At least the mind can say it must be layered, appealing to different levels of the soul.

Now this painting could easily be described as just a lick of paint on a big piece of canvas. Yet right from the beginning I was drawn to it, my eyes not leaving the canvas for at least 15 minutes. My association mechanisms were running wild until my mind shut down and something else took over, something more primal, something that couldn't be measured.

This painting was speaking to me. It was saying something to my soul directly, something about life and death, although I don't know exactly what, not in words anyway, and it didn't matter. For who cares about words when a brief crack of light unveils the Mystery of the Universe.

Nearly twenty years later, there was a Rothko exhibition at the *Gemeentemuseum* (now called Kunstmuseum) in The Hague, which is a short walk from my adoptive mother's house and the area where I grew up. The overview of Rothko's work was on the first floor, while on the ground floor there was an overview exhibition from members of De Stijl, most notably Mondrian and Gerrit Rietveld, the architect, furniture designer, and name giver to the very art school I attended. First, I went to the Rothko exhibition which was spread over six rooms. It was interesting to see his development, his early experiments going from figurative to abstract.

Mondrian had a similar development a generation earlier and the curator was trying to show just that by juxtaposing the two in one room. It seemed a strange choice to me, to have Mondrian's final masterpiece, *Victory Boogie-Woogie*, a jazzy colourful representation of Manhattan and the World War II allies' victory that seemed imminent opposite a small, average Rothko. Before Mondrian went to New York, and before he started his abstract phase, he underwent a spiritual transformation which can be seen in some of his work, most notably *Evolution*, a triptych of a female figure undergoing something that seems like a mixture of melancholy, geometry and enlightenment, perhaps one of my most favourite paintings. After that, he had that *'tree-transforming-into-its-essence-of-lines'* phase. Somewhere in between these transformations, Mondrian not only looked for a way to reduce forms and colours to their essence, but also for a way of expressing basic existential and spiritual emotions that get somewhat lost in his later abstract work.

At the entrance of the room where the two paintings were hanging next to each other it said that Rothko actually didn't appreciate Mondrian's work. Whether the two actually met (Mondrian died just before the end of the war in 1944), and if Rothko had ever seen Mondrian's earlier work, I don't know. It doesn't matter anyway, as the two artists are very different, even though both have been called 'spiritual' at some phase in their lives. What struck me though was that Rothko only really 'got loose' after Mondrian's death, after the war. What did he think of the Holocaust, as a Jew who left Europe behind as a child? What did he think of the fact that none of that world existed anymore? Is it possible that somehow, when words fail, and pictures are just pictures, the souls of those that perished live on in their art?

Ultimately Mark Rothko committed suicide in 1970, a few days before I was born. He didn't leave a note, just his work.

Bullies in the park

Not too long ago – in the age of eternity – when I was a kid, about 9 years old, I was walking on clouds. I wanted to reach the sky you see, and now and then I got pretty close. Every day I walked to school through the Vondel Park in Amsterdam with my friend Clifford.

On entering the park we had to pass the giant tree, then walk along the long lane, across the rose gardens, and over the bridges and ponds. Grownups had to be avoided at all costs, which included my older brother – except perhaps when needed in case of an ambush by bullies (which incidentally could have included Clifford's older sister and her friends).

Clifford's parents were American, and his home was not far from mine. He was living with his mom and older sister. His dad was not there, just like mine, but now and then his dad would visit from New York, which in my mind was nothing less than a Metropolis, home of skyscrapers, monorails, and flying cars. Clifford and I used to play with electronics, like gluing a bunch of batteries and a radio antenna together to function as a walkie-talkie, with a vocal reach of about two metres.

These creations didn't protect us from the bullies, so next to our technological inventions we resorted to using a much more powerful medium, that of our imagination in the shape of our self-made comic books. In the absence of a photocopier, we hand-drew each little book about the adventures of Little Johnny, going to the moon, to the sea, travelling into the past or into the future, all for the stunning price of ten cents a copy.

Not that it had much effect on the bullies either, but boy did our creations make us feel invincible. So much so that one day, whilst walking to school, overthinking our next adventure, I noticed that the ground underneath my feet was slowly but surely descending and I was floating with my head in the clouds, despite the sunny day.

Many years later I heard that Clifford died in a traffic incident in Miami, Florida. I like to think he has clouds under his feet for real

...AND THAT GUY THERE LOOKS LIKE HE
WEARS HIS WIFE'S PANTS WHEN
SHE IS AWAY...

8

From Kings Cross to Eternity

The 7/7 2005 London bombings
My experience

Surviving 7/7

Written in Haarlem on the 10th anniversary

It has been 10 years since that fatal Thursday morning of the 7th of July, 2005 in London when one of four Islamic suicide bombers blew himself up in the Piccadilly Line metro. Approximately 100 feet beneath the ground, between Kings Cross and Russell Square station, I and about a thousand other people were thrown into a silent darkness, and left clinging to life.

It was a morning like most others. I was a bit late getting up and going to work. The night before, London was celebrating being selected as the host for the Olympics in 2012, still seven innocent years away. I had gone for drinks with my colleagues after work in Richmond, and got home fairly late.

After the alarm went off the next morning, I still snoozed for at least half an hour. My recurring flying dream was slowly fading away and I went into my routine of showering and then breakfast with Ailish. She was the reason I found myself in London.

On that day, she was preparing for a weekend trip to Berlin. Just like any other day, we kissed each other goodbye and I went on my way, walking towards the nearest Tube station at Caledonian Road.

As a newcomer from little Holland, these inner London journeys were always like a mini-adventure: so many people, so many impressions, the rhythm, the energy. But as I arrived at the station that day, the gate had a little note on it saying that the station was closed due to maintenance or something.

This was before smartphones and travel apps, but I knew enough of my journey to go for the alternative: taking the bus to the next station. Any bus would do, and soon enough a double-decker arrived that was going towards Kings Cross Station.

Busy as it was, I stayed right at the front of the lower deck next to the driver, taking in the view of the commuting Londoners. Knowing I would be too late to work now, I embraced the situation, letting myself be guided by the flow of the traffic.

Arriving at the chaotic twin stations of Kings Cross and Saint Pancras, I passed down the first set of steps where I got a copy of the free Metro newspaper and quickly made my way further down the large escalator towards the damp platforms.

My line was the *Piccadilly Line*, the dark blue line with the funny name. I needed to take it in the direction of Heathrow Airport via Earl's Court where I had to make a transfer. But first I entered the platform.

Man, it was busy. I went all the way to the front end of the platform in the hope of getting a place in the train when it arrived, but had to let two pass by as they were way too busy, packed with commuters like sweaty sardines in a tin can. Without any logic I decided to go all the way to the other end of the platform, to get into the back end of the train, hoping that it would be slightly less busy. Little did I know, that decision would actual-ly save my life. I walked along the  platform, unknowingly passing some guy with a bulging ruck-sack. I managed to board the next train and just like that, it left the platform and pounded into the dark, enclosed tunnel.

All I know is something happened in that tunnel that ex-tended reality.

..

As the train pulled out of Kings Cross Station, I observed the overly crowded carriage; even an average commute in London never fails to provide some great people watch-ing opportunities. The crowd was so diverse and energetic, so alive. It was too busy to read my Metro, which I kept under my arm, but I was content to just look around and daydream.

While we rumbled along together, there was suddenly a

muted sound, a hollowed-out bang, and it resonated through the tunnel into our carriage for about eight seconds. The chatter in the carriage immediately stopped, followed shortly by the train itself, and ultimately the lights.

For an infinite moment there was darkness and silence.

I was frozen to the ground, yet I was fully conscious.

At first, my mind went into overdrive, but before I could materialise a thought, the emergency lights went on. My fellow passengers re-emerged in a different light, and it was as if they were characters in a play with the stage curtains closing and opening again, and now they had different masks on: masks of confusion, fear and yet, silence. The train was now fully at a standstill. Slowly but surely, the compartment started filling with smoke.

Some disaster films come close, but this movie now playing in front of me was pretty bad.
'Jesus Christ Oh Jesus!' a woman started yelling next to me while she went down on her knees.
'Jesus Oh Lord Christ' another person yelled after her, and within seconds, a palpable layer of panic was added to the blurry smoke in the carriage.
'Help me please God help me!' someone cried in vain.
'Open the door!! Can anyone open the fucking door?!' some guy yelled from somewhere in the front of the carriage. I was 5-10 metres away from the very end of the train and could see a guy desperately trying to open the back door, in vain.

The Tube is called *'the Tube'* for a reason; smashing in windows is pointless as all that does is unveil the wall.

But at least it would give air, so another guy was trying to smash in a window with the back of his shoe but only hurt himself in the process.

'I don't want to die!' a voice yelled in the now thick layer of dark smoke that had ascended at head-height. I couldn't breathe. Some instinct told me to bend my knees and go and sit on the ground. As I went down, I realised I was not the only one. Strangely, there seemed to be a place of hope at foot level under the blanket of smoke. I could see other people sitting, laying down over each other, some talking, but not for long as the smoke got heavier, and heavier, and heavier.

'This is it,' I thought, 'just like my grandfather's parents; being killed with a bunch of strangers screaming in an enclosed space without oxygen …'

'This is it.' I closed my eyes –

.

.

.

.

.

Ailish, who was still on her way to Berlin via Luton, suddenly showed up, somewhere in between my vision, my mind, and my soul. I wanted to talk to her, but my words failed to reach her. Her image told me something, without words; she didn't want me to go away. Next, I saw her drifting away from me, floating in a black void, all alone, looking scared, surrounded by nothing.

Ultimately, she disappeared. The thought of her being gone, not me, made me yell out: *'Noooo!!'*

Now it was at that very moment, that infinitely undefinable moment, that something intervened. A voice without sound told me that it would be all right.

I open my eyes and the smoke had stabilised above foot level. I could breathe. Barely, but just enough. Then a real voice sounded through the carriage: *'A note is being passed down from the front of the train saying help is on its way. They forced the doors open and are releasing the passengers!!'*

The masks of the actors around me instantly changed and a resounding group cheer erupted *'Yaaay!!'*

Still sitting, the smoke slowly faded and I could see the people closest to me more clearly. One guy with a bottle of water was holding on to his blackened face. It was then that I noticed my throat felt cork dry and I asked him for a sip. With a smile he gave me his bottle and I took the most thankful sip I could imagine.

Words were being exchanged. The sound of shuffling indicated some movement, and with the same instinct I rose up again. It is unbelievable how in England the art form of queuing is perfected; everybody neatly got in line to slowly leave the compartment.

Walking from carriage to carriage the drama became more and more apparent. After about four or five carriages, there was finally someone vaguely official-looking with an orange vest and plastic yellow helmet. Like a saviour of the underground, he guided everyone step by step to the outside of the train, next to the rails. We were helped down onto the ground by another angel in orange.

The otherwise dark and murky tunnel was lit with safety lamps. There must have been an impact further up the train. There was a strange smell of melted iron and burnt flesh that prompted me to look the other way, and I continued on my path.

I could hear people talking, and I could see one guy taking pictures. I suddenly realised I had my phone in my trouser pocket, but of course there was no reception underground. Next to me was a woman with a deeply traumatised expression, her tears washing away some of the soot on her face. I shared a moment of silence with her as we walked along.

That march of the living dead lasted seemingly forever, until, well, what else can I say, there was light at the end of the tunnel.

The light turned out to be Kings Cross Station again, with more angels on the elevated platform, extending me the friendliest of *'You aw' right mate?'* greetings, in the history of greetings. I responded with relieved mumbles and headed towards

the escalator. They didn't work and I stood still for a moment at the foot of it, admiring the sunlight coming from above.

I am alive.

Upstairs at street level was a whole other world. The bright light. The noise of people yelling, ambulances and helicopters. Water! Pallets of water! I took a bottle and drank it in one gulp. People kept asking me things, but I just wanted to talk to Ailish.

My phone! I flipped it open. Battery dead!! Of course!

More people asked me questions, but all I wanted was to be back home and use a phone. I started walking. It is about a

half hour walk from Kings Cross back to Holloway and before I knew it, I was already halfway. More helicopters were in the sky and sirens were blaring. I was functioning on pure adrenaline, and as I walked along, I passed a shop window and I saw my own reflection for the first time. My face was completely black! I continued walking, running now and then, coughing up weird black stuff. I could still smell it, the burning ... I felt the need to cry but ran even faster now.

'I am home!' I yelled upon entering the house, hoping any of our other housemates were there, but I was only greeted by silence. I threw down my jacket, covered in black soot, and walked towards the house phone, turning on the TV on my way. It showed the very place where I had just come from, and for the first time, news about the explosions came in. Not technical faults or coincidences. This was planned and calculated.

Ailish's phone made a non-connecting sound. I walked towards the bathroom and now saw more clearly how dark and bruised I look. I tried to wash my face and spit out an endless stream of soot.

This time the phone made a connecting sound ...

26 people were killed on the Piccadilly Line that day, as were 26 more on the other three target sites, with countless others injured.

Amsterdam Central Station

Life

Ego
Fury
Rage
Anger
Anxiety
Frustration
Depression
Expectations
Caged energy
Disappointment

Letting go

Responsibility
Commitment
Compassion
Imagination
Empathy
Meaning
Purpose
Spirit
Flow
Love

Live

9
From Me to You

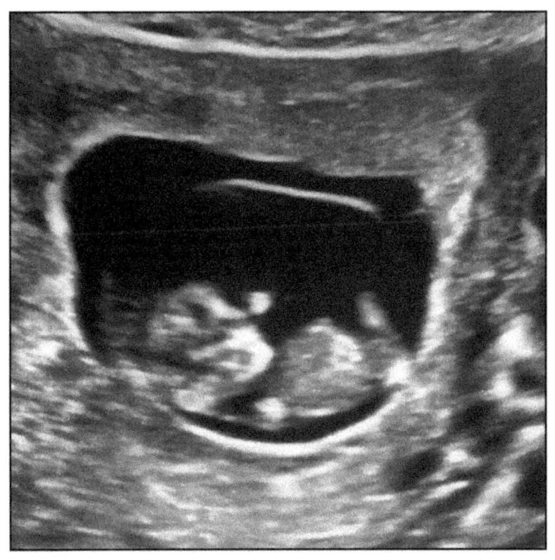

echo 26/09/2017

2018 - present
Breaking the cycle

Full of Joy

Yaron

Hebrew: יָרוֹן

meaning: *'is/will be full of joy'*
or *'to shout, to sing'*

Haarlem,
Thursday, 25 June 2020

Dear Yaron,

Welcome to the world my lovely son. At two years, you seem to have a strong will of your own. Like your mother, you are operating independently just fine. God only knows who you will become, but whatever the result, know that I love you.

I trust you will be able to find your you, your path, your calling, your occupation or whatever it will be that you value in life, your love in and for life.

Also, you have a curious mind, just like your dad, and that's why I'd like to tell you about the world, where you come from, your background, and what you could learn from all this.

By the time you read this, you might already have realised that life isn't always fair. You can't always get what you want, the Stones song goes. That is, if you know what you want. Just stay active and things will come your way.

My hope is that you will be spared the bad luck that so many of us endure. There are plenty of good things, even a few great things, in this life.

I cherish the fact you can walk around this Earth and smell freshly mown grass, eat an apple, or pancakes with golden syrup, listen to music that makes your spine go funny and be in love for the very first time, making you walk on clouds.

Dream out loud.
Think a little, love a lot.
Keep on smiling.

Tomorrow is going to be an early start. Another hot one. Perhaps the last one for a while. A *daddy day*. I will prepare the little swimming pool for you, I know you have been enjoying them so much the last few days.

Sleep well, as you are now. *Shhhhh.*

Love,

Pappie

$1 + 1 = 3$

We are sitting at the dining table, Ailish, Yaron and I. It is a grey, wet, windy day in March. Yaron had a full day at school followed by after-school care club, where he was absorbed in a game of table football when I collected him..

Ailish and I are trying to get him to talk about his day, but instead he just smiles, his lip curling like Elvis, the way it has since he was one month old. He utters the words 'poop fart' before counting from 1 to 20, half in English, half in Dutch, and eats his cracker with cream cheese.

Ailish and I are talking, as we have been doing since the day we met. Yaron declares he is 'done!' and suddenly jumps off his chair and cleans his mouth and hands with a wet wipe. 'But don't you want some yoghurt with honey?' Ailish asks Yaron, and immediately he goes back to his chair and says 'yes please mummy' in an English accent. He eats the yoghurt and squints his eyes. Ever the actor.

It is nice and warm inside and it occurs to me how happy and content Yaron is, so self-assured at this young age – such a contrast to how alienated I had often felt as a child. And how confused and lost I can sometimes feel as an adult. Outside, a pandemic is raging. There is terrorism, political divisions, stress, Parkinson's Disease.

But none of it matters. We are together. All that matters is here and now. There is no logic, no reason. Just *this*.

Us three.

10

Full Circle

Phantom Parents

Most people have two parents, I have four. Or eight, if I include *their* partners. Normally the saying goes: 'You don't choose their parents'. Well, I *do.*

Like everyone, I have parents who *made* me. They broke up even before I was born. And then I was relinquished.

I have parents who *adopted* me; *chose* me. They loved me. They wanted me. Then they broke up. One died too soon. But I was still raised with unconditional love.

Despite this, I have always felt... disconnected. The experience of being adopted left me with an uprooted feeling, a hunger for connection, recognition, belonging. "Who am I? Where do I come from? *Who are my parents?*"

When I was a child, my parents were *phantoms*; a mystery that would get lost in my imagination:

My (absent) father was a king of a remote kingdom whose son went missing, whose return was eagerly awaited.

My (absent) mother was a strangely familiar yet alien being that would show up now and then , and then leave again.

My (present) mother was a loving soul full of laughter but also a walking database and a feeding machine to rebel against.

My (occasionally present) father was an ephemeral spirit, living in my heart.

Finally, as an adult, I created my own 'family', like a band, or a tribe. But my instinct is to fight 'belonging' as much as it craves it. This is the paradox. Like living in an Escher illustration.

Only very recently, whilst working on this book, I came across many other adoptees' stories and felt a sense of belonging, connection, and recognition that I hardly knew I was missing.

At the same time, I am faced with raising my own son; my own flesh and blood. Just under two years ago, when he was only two years old, I was diagnosed with *Young Onset Parkinson's Disease*, which explains years of battling with my mood and energy.

Will I be a good father to him? Will I be 'me' ... ? Or will *I* be a *phantom parent...?*

Life is a work in progress, and no one knows what is in stock, but thanks to my diagnosis I have a sense of urgency in life; a newfound strength, and a commitment to love the two people that are most dear to me: *Ailish and Yaron.*

I think that'll work.

PHOTO: MYRA MAY

Not The End
(To Be Continued)

Resources

Adoption: The Making of Me
Podcast/YouTube by- and with adoptees.
I will be their guest summer 2023.
www.adoptionthemakingofme.com

Who Am I...Really?
Adoptees share their adoption journeys & attempts
at reunion with biological family members.
www.whoamireallypodcast.com

Jewish Monument
Online database of the Dutch Holocaust victims,
including the Enker family.
www.joodsmonument.nl

My Website
Contains background information, artwork, blog,
work portfolio, links and much more.
www.davidenker.com

Acknowledgements

199

Thank you

Pieter & Iljoesja, Edgar & Ines, Alex Berendsen,
Shona Brethouwer, Rebecca van Leeuwen,
Maureen & Michael, Sean, Claire, Alan, Andrew, Rebecca,
Laura Meeuwesse, Randolph,
Hannah Huber, Kristin Anderson, Lisa Hall,
Piet, Anne, Joost, Daniël, Alwine, Joop, Florian,
Selma, Marc, Daphne,
Rogier, Marleen,
Ineke,
Ailish & Yaron.